THE (.Y

S. ....

 AL Rowse

Edited by A.L. Rowse

King Lear

Modern Text
with Introduction

UNIVERSITY PRESS OF AMERICA

Copyright © 1984 by A.L. Rowse

University Press of America,™ Inc.

4720 Boston Way
Lanham, MD 20706

3 Henrietta Street
London WC2E 8LU England

Distributed to the trade by The Scribner Book Companies

Library of Congress Cataloging in Publication Data

Shakespeare, William, 1564-1616.
  King Lear.

  (The Contemporary Shakespeare)
  I. Rowse, A.L. (Alfred Leslie), 1903-
II. Title. III. Series: Shakespeare, William, 1564-1616.
Plays (University Press of America : Pbk. ed.)
PR2819.A2R68   1984   822.3'3   84-15388
ISBN 0-8191-3911-4 (pbk.)

This play is also available as part of Volume II in a six volume clothbound
and slipcased set.

Book design by Leon Bolognese

WHY A CONTEMPORARY SHAKESPEARE?

The starting point of my project was when I learned both from television and in education, that Shakespeare is being increasingly dropped in schools and colleges because of the difficulty of the language. In some cases, I gather, they are given just a synopsis of the play, then the teacher or professor embroiders from his notes.

This is deplorable. We do not want Shakespeare progressively dropped because of superfluous difficulties that can be removed, skilfully, conservatively, keeping to every line of the text Nor must we look at the question statically, for this state of affairs will worsen as time goes on and we get further away from the language of 400 years ago—difficult enough in all conscience now.

We must begin by ridding our mind of prejudice, i.e. we must not pre-judge the matter. A friend of mine on New York radio said that he was 'appalled' at the very idea; but when he heard my exposition of what was proposed he found it reasonable and convincing.

Just remember, I do not need it myself: *I live in the Elizabethan age*, Shakespeare's time, and have done for years, and am familiar with its language, and his. But even for me there are still difficulties—still more for modern people, whom I am out to help.

Who, precisely?

Not only students at school and in college, but all readers of Shakespeare. Not only those, but all viewers of the plays, in the theatre, on radio and television— actors too, who increasingly find pronunciation of the words difficult, particularly obsolete ones—and there are many, besides the difficulty of accentuation.

The difficulties are naturally far greater for non-English-speaking peoples. We must remember that he is our greatest asset, and that other peoples use him a great deal in learning our language. There are no Iron Curtains for him—though, during Mao's Cultural Revolution in China, he was prohibited. Now that the ban has been lifted, I learn that the Chinese in thousands flock to his plays.

Now, a good deal that was grammatical four hundred years ago is positively ungrammatical today. We might begin by removing what is no longer good grammar.

For example: plural subjects with a verb in the singular:

'*Is* Bushy, Green and the earl of Wiltshire dead?' Any objection to replacing 'is' correctly by 'are'? Certainly not. I notice that some modern editions already correct—

These high wild hills and rough uneven ways

Draws out our miles and makes them wearisome

to 'draw' and 'make', quite sensibly. Then, why not go further and regularise this Elizabethan usage to modern, consistently throughout?

Similarly with archaic double negatives—'Nor shall you not think neither'—and double comparatives: 'this is more worser than before.' There are hundreds of instances of what is now just bad grammar to begin with.

There must be a few thousand instances of superfluous subjunctives to reduce to simplicity and sense. Today we use the subjunctive occasionally after 'if', when we say 'if it be'. But we mostly say today 'if it is'. Now Shakespeare has hundreds of subjunctives, not only after if, but after though, although, unless, lest, whether, until, till, etc.

I see no point whatever in retaining them. They only add superfluous trouble in learning English, when the great appeal of our language as a world-language is precisely that it has less grammar to learn than almost any. Russian is unbelievably complicated. Inflected languages—German is like Latin in this respect—are really rather backward; it has been a great recommendation that English has been more progressive in this respect in simplifying itself.

Now we can go further along this line: keep a few subjunctives, if you must, but reduce them to a minimum.

Let us come to the verb. It is a great recommendation to modern English that our verbs are comparatively simple to conjugate—unlike even French, for example. In the Elizabethan age there was a great deal more of it, and some of it inconsistent in modern usage. Take Shakespeare's,

'Where is thy husband now? Where be thy brothers?'

Nothing is lost by rendering this as we should today:

Where is your husband now? Where are your brothers?

And so on.

The second and third person singular—all those shouldsts and wouldsts, wilts and shalts, haths and doths, have become completely obsolete. Here a vast simplification may be effected—with no loss as far as I can see, and with advantages from several points of view.

For example, 'st' at the end of a word is rather difficult to say, and more difficult even for us when it is succeeded by a word beginning with 'th'. Try saying, 'Why usurpedst thou this?' Foreigners have the greatest difficulty in pronouncing our 'th' anyway—many never succeed in getting it round their tongues. Many of these tongue-twisters even for us proliferate in Shakespeare, and I see no objection to getting rid of *superfluous* difficulties. Much easier for people to say, 'Why did you usurp this?'—the same number of syllables too.

This pre-supposes getting rid of almost all thous and thees and thines. I have no objection to keeping a few here and there, if needed for a rhyme—even then they are sometimes not necessary.

Some words in Shakespeare have changed their meaning into the exact opposite: we ought to remove that stumbling-block. When Hamlet says, 'By heaven, I'll make a ghost of him that *lets* me', he means *stops*; and we should replace it by stops, or holds me. Shakespeare regularly uses the word 'owe' where we should say own: the meaning has changed. Take a line like, 'Thou dost here usurp the name thou ow'st not': we should say, 'You do here usurp the name you own not', with the bonus of getting rid of two ugly 'sts'.

The word 'presently' in the Elizabethan age did not mean in a few minutes or so, but immediately—instantly has the same number of syllables. 'Prevent' then had its Latin meaning, to go before, or forestall. Shakespeare frequently uses the word 'still' for always or ever.

Let us take the case of many archaic forms of words, simple one-syllable words that can be replaced without the slightest difference to the scansion: 'sith' for since, 'wrack' for wreck, 'holp' for helped, 'writ' for wrote, 'brake' for broke, 'spake' for spoke, 'bare' for bore, etc.

These give no trouble, nor do a lot of other words that he uses: 'repeal' for recall, 'reproof' for disproof, 'decline' for incline. A few words do give more trouble. The linguistic scholar, C. T. Onions, notes that it is sometimes difficult to give the precise meaning Shakespeare attaches to the word 'conceit'; it usually means thought, or fancy, or concept. I do not know that it ever has our meaning; actually the word 'conceited' with him means ingenious or fantastic, as 'artificial' with Elizabethans meant artistic or ingenious.

There is a whole class of words that have completely gone out, of which moderns do not know the meaning. I find no harm in replacing the word 'coistrel' by rascal, which is what it means—actually it has much the same sound—or 'coil' by fuss; we find 'accite' for summon, 'indigest' for formless. Hamlet's word 'reechy', for the incestuous kisses of his mother and her brother-in-law, has gone out of use: the nearest word, I suppose, would be reeky, but filthy would be a suitable modern equivalent.

In many cases it is extraordinary how little one would need to change, how conservative one could be. Take Hamlet's famous soliloquy, 'To be or not to be.' I find only two words that moderns would not know the meaning of, and one of those we might guess:

> . . .When he himself might his *quietus* make
> With a bare bodkin? Who would *fardels* bear. . .

'Quietus' means put paid; Elizabethans wrote the Latin 'quietus est' at the bottom of a bill that was paid—when it was—to say that it was settled. So that you could replace 'quietus' by settlement, same number of syllables, though not the same accentuation; so I would prefer to use the word acquittance, which has both.

'Fardels' means burdens; I see no objection to rendering, 'Who would burdens bear'—same meaning, same number of syllables, same accent: quite simple. I expect all the ladies to know what a bodkin is: a long pin, or skewer.

Now let us take something really difficult—perhaps the most difficult passage to render in all Shakespeare. It is the virtuoso comic piece describing all the diseases that horseflesh is heir to, in *The Taming of the Shrew*. The horse is Petruchio's. President Reagan tells me that this is the one Shakespearean part that he played—and a very gallant one too. In Britain last year we saw a fine performance of his on horseback in Windsor Park along-side of Queen Elizabeth II—very familiar ground to William Shakespeare and Queen Elizabeth I, as we know from *The Merry Wives of Windsor*.

Here is a headache for us: Petruchio's horse (not President Reagan's steed) was 'possessed with the glanders, and like to mose in the chine; troubled with the lampass, infected with the fashions, full of windgalls, sped with spavins, rayed with the yellows, past cure of the fives, stark spoiled with the staggers, begnawn with the bots; swayed in the back, and shoulder-shotten; near-legged before, and with a half-cheeked bit, and a headstall of sheep's leather', etc.

What on earth are we to make of that? No doubt it raised a laugh with Elizabethans, much more familiarly acquainted with horseflesh than we are; but I doubt if Hollywood was able to produce a nag for Reagan that qualified in all these respects.

Now, even without his horsemanship, we can clear one fence at the outset: 'mose in the chine'. Pages of superfluous commentary have been devoted to that word 'mose'. There was no such Elizabethan word: it was simply a printer's misprint for 'mourn', meaning dripping or running; so it suggests a running sore. You would need to consult the *Oxford English Dictionary*, compiled on historical lines, for some of the words, others like 'glanders' country folk know and we can guess.

So I would suggest a rendering something like this: 'possessed with glanders, and with a running sore in the back; troubled in the gums, and infected in the glands; full of galls in the fetlocks and swollen in the joints; yellow with jaundice, past cure of the strangles; stark spoiled with the staggers, and gnawed by worms; swayed in the back and shoulder put out; near-legged before, and with a half-cheeked bit and headgear of sheep's leather', etc. That at least makes it intelligible.

Oddly enough, one encounters the greatest difficulty with the least important words and phrases, Elizabethan expletives and malapropisms, or salutations like God 'ild you, Godden, for God shield you, Good-even, and so on. 'God's wounds' was Elizabeth I's favourite swearword; it appears frequently enough in Victorian novels as 'Zounds'— I have never heard anyone use it. The word 'Marry!', as in the phrase 'Marry come up!' has similarly gone out, though a very old gentleman at All Souls, Sir Charles Oman, had heard the phrase in the back-streets of Oxford just after the 1914-18 war. 'Whoreson' is frequent on the lips of coarse fellows in Shakespeare: the equivalent in Britain today would be bloody, in America (I suppose) s.o.b.

Relative pronouns, who and which: today we use who for persons, which for things. In Elizabethan times the two were hardly distinguished and were interchangeable. Provokingly Shakespeare used the personal relative 'who' more frequently for impersonal objects, rivers, buildings, towns; and then he no less frequently uses 'which' for persons. This calls out to be regularised for the modern reader.

Other usages are more confusing. The word 'cousin'

was used far more widely by the Elizabethans for their
kin: it included nephews, for instance. Thus it is confusing in the English History plays to find a whole lot of
nephews—like Richard III's, whom he had made away
with in the Tower of London—referred to and addressed
as cousins. That needs regularisation today, in the in-
terests of historical accuracy and to get the relationship
clear. The word 'niece' was sometimes used of a grand-
child—in fact this is the word Shakespeare used in his
will for his little grand-daughter Elizabeth, his eventual
heiress who ended up as Lady Barnard, leaving money to
her poor relations the Hathaways at Stratford. The Latin
word *neptis*, from which niece comes also meant grand-
child—Shakespeare's grammar-school education at Stratford was in Latin, and this shows you that he often
thought of a word in terms of its Latin derivation.

Malapropisms, misuse of words, sometimes mistaking
of meanings, are frequent with uneducated people, and
sometimes not only with those. Shakespeare transcribed
them from lower-class life to raise a laugh, more frequently than any writer for the purpose. They are an
endearing feature of the talk of Mistress Quickly, hostess
of the Boar's Inn in East Cheapside, and we have no difficulty in making out what she means. But in case some of
us do, and for the benefit of non-native English speakers,
I propose the correct word in brackets afterwards: 'You
have brought her into such a canaries [quandary]. . .and
she's as fartuous [virtuous] a civil, modest wife. . .'

Abbreviations: Shakespeare's text is starred—and in
my view, marred—by innumerable abbreviations, which
not only look ugly on the page but are sometimes difficult to pronounce. It is not easy to pronounce 'is't', or
'in't', or 'on't', and some others: if we cannot get rid of
them altogether they should be drastically reduced.
Similarly with 'i'th'', 'o'th'', with which the later plays
are liberally bespattered, for "in the" or "of the."

We also have a quite unnecessary spattering of apostrophes in practically all editions of the plays—''d' for the past participle, e.g. 'gather'd'. Surely it is much better to regularise the past participle 'ed', e.g. gathered; and when the last syllable is, far less frequently, to be pronounced, then accent it, gatherèd.

This leads into the technical question of scansion, where a practising poet is necessary to get the accents right, to help the reader, and still more the actor. Most people will hardly notice that, very often, the frequent ending of words in 'ion', like reputation, has to be pronounced with two syllables at the end. So I propose to accent this when necessary, e.g. reputatiòn. I have noticed the word 'ocean' as tri-syllabic, so I accent it, to help, oceàn. A number of words which to us are monosyllables were pronounced as two: hour, fire, tired; I sometimes accent or give them a dieresis, either hoùr or fïre. In New England speech words like prayèr, thère, are apt to be pronounced as two syllables—closer to Elizabethan usage (as with words like gotten) than is modern speech in Britain.

What I notice in practically all editions of Shakespeare's plays is that the editors cannot be relied on to put the accents in the right places. One play edited by a well known Shakespearean editor had, I observed, a dozen accents placed over the wrong syllables. This is understandable, for these people don't write poetry and do not know how to scan. William Shakespeare knew all about scanning, and you need to be both familiar with Elizabethan usage and a practising traditional poet to be able to follow him.

His earlier verse was fairly regular in scansion, mostly iambic pentameter with a great deal of rhyme. As time went on he loosened out, until there are numerous irregular lines—this leaves us much freer in the matter of modernising. Our equivalents should be rhythmically as close as possible, but a strait-jacket need be no part of the equipment. A good Shakespearean scholar tells us, 'there is no necessity for Shakespeare's lines to scan absolutely. He thought of his verse as spoken rather than written and of his rhythmic units in terms of the voice rather than the page.'

There is nothing exclusive or mandatory about my project. We can all read Shakespeare in any edition we like—in the rebarbative olde Englishe spelling of the First Folio, if we wish. Any number of conventional academic editions exist, all weighed down with a burden of notes, many of them superfluous. I propose to make most of them unnecessary—only one occasionally at the foot of very few pages. Let the text be freed of superfluous difficulties, remove obstacles to let it speak for itself, while adhering conservatively to every line.

We really do not need any more editions of the Plays on conventional lines—more than enough of those exist already. But *A Contemporary Shakespeare* on these lines—both revolutionary and conservative—should be a help to everybody all round the world—though especially for younger people, increasingly with time moving away from the language of 400 years ago.

INTRODUCTION

King Lear and *Hamlet* are the twin peaks of Shakespeare's achievement and therefore, we may say,
in world drama. *King Lear* was written in 1606,
some five or six years after *Hamlet*, with which it is in
marked contrast. One similarity they share, though the
treatment again is different: the theme, the use, of
madness—always exciting on the stage, as Shakespeare
early learned from Kyd's *The Spanish Tragedy*, and put
to use in his own first tragedy, *Titus Andronicus*. Other-
wise, all is in contrast. Hamlet is an introspective character, exploring interior depths, acutely self-conscious
and self-questioning of his own motives and actions,
everything. King Lear is ignorant of himself and others—
'you should not have been old till you had been wise';
the play depicts his progress to knowledge and humility,
through the tribulations and suffering his kingly unwis-
dom had brought down upon him. He always retains a
regal dignity through all the indignities and follies.

These are externalised, into the world of nature, the
batterings of storm and tempest, homelessness and
heartlessness. *King Lear* is extensive, revealing a world
full of evil and conflict; *Hamlet* is intensive: Hamlet's
burden is imposed upon him from without—as in
Greek tragedy—through no fault of his own: our sympathy with him is the greater, for Lear brought his

tragedy upon his own head, needlessly. People do, however; our sympathy gradually grows, with him, throughout this epic play to its terrible end, with the death of his innocent daughter, Cordelia.

In the old play of *King Lear*, which was Shakespeare's point of departure, this did not happen: it was the extremism of his imagination that inflicted this upon us—which the kind heart of Dr. Johnson could not endure. Perhaps Shakespeare's rigorous artistic intuition felt that, after all the agony of mind and the horrors all endure in various ways from the inherent tragedy of man's life on earth, this utter desolation was the only possible conclusion that was in keeping. There are other horrors, like the putting-out of Gloucester's eyes—and such things occur today—which Dr. Johnson's heart found unendurable. However, he too knew the ills of life, which is what the play is about, and braces us with a secondary consideration: 'let it be remembered that our author well knew what would please the audience for which he wrote.' The play was performed at Court before King James I on Innocents' Day, 26 December 1606.

Most qualified critics confess themselves defeated by so epic a work—Hazlitt, for example, in a fine phrase: 'all that we can say must fall far short of the subject, or even what we ourselves conceive of it.' Precisely—here is the best of reasons for letting the work speak for itself, not burden it with discussions and commentaries unworthy of it. Charles Lamb was defeated too, and thought that, from its sheer scale, it is impossible of representation on the stage. But this is wrong; we must remind ourselves—to adapt a phrase of Gertrude Stein (a good Shakespearean)—that a play is a play is a play. The best way to retain a sense of proportion is to see it, as Dr. Johnson did, in contemporary terms and in the context of Shakespeare's work.

One theme to which he draws our attention is this. 'In Shakespeare's best plays there is generally some peculiar prevailing folly that runs through the whole piece. In *Lear* the dotages of judicial astrology are severely ridiculed. I fancy—was the date of its first performance well considered—it would be found that something or other happened at that time which gave a more than ordinary run to this deceit.' Several passages give point to this. 'This is the excellent foppery of the world that, when we are sick in fortune—often the surfeits of our own behaviour—we make guilty of our own disasters the sun, the moon, and stars. As if we were villains on necessity; fools by heavenly compulsion; knaves, thieves, and traitors by spherical predominance; drunkards, liars, and adulterers by an enforced obedience of planetary influence. An admirable evasion of whoremaster man to lay his goatish disposition to the charge of a star.' And he gives instances.

Gloucester's view is that 'these late eclipses of the sun and moon portend no good to us.' He registers 'the sequent effects: love cools, friendship falls off, brothers divide. In cities, mutinies; in countries *i.e. counties*, discord; in palaces, treason; and the bond cracked betwixt son and father.' Johnson's perception was perfectly justified, though he did not know the facts: there were eclipses of both sun and moon in September and October 1605. The time was full of astrological and demonological discussion, taken up contemporaneously into *Macbeth*, and into the crazy talk among Lear, the Fool and Edgar feigning mad in the storm with his assumed fear of the fiends pursuing him. Their strange names come from Samuel Harsnet's *Declaration of*

Egregious Popish Impostures of 1603, an exposure of experiences of hysteria actually induced by Catholic priests pretending to exorcise these fiends from some credulous women.[1]

Other features of contemporary life occur: a vivid description of the beggars who roamed the country,

> who, with roaring voices,
> Strike in their numbed and mortified bare arms
> Pins, wooden pricks, nails, sprigs of rosemary—

as in India or the Middle East today. Edgar describes characteristics of serving-men, pretending to have been one: 'proud in heart and mind; that curled my hair; wore gloves in my cap; swore as many oaths as I spoke words and broke them; one that slept in the contriving of lust, and waked to it.' No illusions about anybody, of whatever class or station—regular with Shakespeare.

The stage itself has its reference as usual: 'pat he comes like the catastrophe of the old comedy'—how familiar and professional! 'My cue is villainous melancholy, with a sigh like Tom o'Bedlam'—a folklore character, subject of a marvellous, but anonymous, poem of the time. (Who on earth could have written it?) 'O, these eclipses do portend these divisions!' It was the regular thing to put petty common offenders in the stocks; in the porches of country churches we still may see them. For Regan's husband to put her father the King's messenger, the Earl of Kent, in the stocks is thus doubly shocking. Gloucester protests,

> Your purposed low correction
> Is such as basest and contemnedest wretches
> For pilferings and most common trespasses
> Are punished with.

---

[1] cf my *The Elizabethan Renaissance: The Life of the Society*, 264-72.

Elizabethan society knew the proper distinctions between people. It is given to the Fool to speak common
sense about social distinctions: 'he's a mad yeoman
that sees his son a gentleman before him.' The Fool in
Lear is the most remarkable example of the type
throughout Shakespeare: philosophic and reflective, he
counterpoints Lear's folly, brings home to him his
faults and lack of judgment, and has a part in bringing
him to his senses. It was an appropriate role for the actor, distinguished in his own right, Robert Armin—not
a role for Will Kemp, who had left the Company some
years before. *King Lear* does not demand a large cast;
the entirely professional master would suit his
characters to the resources of the Company. No doubt
Burbage played Lear, but what well-trained boy actors
to be able to portray such bitches as Goneril and Regan!

In other versions of the story the king did not go mad.
But a year or two before Shakespeare wrote his play a
suspicious tale came to light. A gentleman servant of
the Queen, one Brian Annesley, became senile. His two
elder daughters tried to get him certified as insane to get
hold of his estate. His youngest daughter, Cordelia,
resisted this, considering that his services 'deserved a
better agnomination than at his last gasp to be recorded
and registered a lunatic.' No reason whatever why
Shakespeare should not have known the story; from
constant performances at Court he would know about
the various officers who served the Queen. And it was
this kind Cordelia who, after the dowager Countess of
Southampton's death, next year married young Sir William Harvey (this is why Thorp, in his Dedication of the
Sonnets, was wishing *his* Mr. W.H., not Shakespeare's, all
happiness and the eternity of having progeny to carry on
his line, the very next year, 1609). The most sensitive
register of the age was one for picking up hints and

suggestions, bits and pieces for his work wherever they were to be found, from life as well as from books.

Taking his story from the old play and from Holinshed, he adapted the underplot of Gloucester and his sons from Sidney's *Arcadia*; one detail, which he put to use for the test when Cordelia properly reserved half of her love for her future husband, was suggested by something he read in Camden's popular *Remains Concerning Britain*, which came out in 1605 the year before the play. It is full of snatches of contemporary songs, ballads, folklore; and has examples of the *sententiae* in rhymed couplets, of which Elizabethans were so fond that they inscribed them everywhere, on their beds, walls, ceilings. For some absurd reason commentators call them 'gnomic verse' and condemn them as bad poetry—but they are utterly characteristic of the age, like epitaphs, or the inscription on his own tombstone. We see him clearly in them:

> Have more than thou showest,
> Speak less than thou knowest,
> Lend less than thou owest,
> Ride more than thou goest [walk]. . .

each one of these adjurations is borne out in his own life.

Nor is he less recognisable in such thoughts as—

> full oft 'tis seen
> Our means secure us, and our mere defects
> Prove our commodities.

He expresses this reflection in various guises several times over—no doubt it was a conclusion from experience. As also—

> Striving to better, oft we mar what's well.

As he grew older his language became grander and grander, more devious, unexpected, unpredictable:

> All blest secrets,

All you unpublished virtues of the earth. . .
          Be aidant and remediate
     In the good man's distress.
We even find a metaphysical 'conceit' such as attracted
poets a generation or two later:
                         There she shook
     The holy water from her heavenly eyes. . .
Politicians get their comeuppance as always—the word
conveyed a pejorative meaning to Elizabethans:
               Get thee glass eyes,
     And, like a scurvy politician, seem
     To see the things you do not.

There is a sense in which we may regard *King Lear*,
along with *Measure for Measure*, as the most philosophic of the plays.

The language of so complex a play exhibits an extraordinary range of expression, with many rare words and
obscurities, which need clarifying for reader, hearer and
actor. This modern text does just this where needful,
conservatively, while adhering to every line of
Shakespeare—the principle adhered to through this
edition.

CHARACTERS

LEAR, King of Britain
GONERIL, Lear's eldest daughter
REGAN, Lear's second daughter
CORDELIA, Lear's youngest daughter
DUKE OF ALBANY, husband of Goneril
DUKE OF CORNWALL, husband of Regan
KING OF FRANCE
DUKE OF BURGUNDY

EARL OF KENT
EARL OF GLOUCESTER
EDGAR, son of Gloucester, later disguised as Poor Tom
EDMUND, bastard son of Gloucester

OSWALD, Goneril's steward
Lear's FOOL
Three KNIGHTS
CURAN, gentleman of Gloucester's household
GENTLEMEN, Three SERVANTS, OLD MAN, a tenant of
Gloucester, Two MESSENGERS, DOCTOR, attendant on
Cordelia, A CAPTAIN, follower of Edmund, HERALD,
Two OFFICERS, Knights of Lear's train, servants,
soldiers, attendants, gentlemen

Act I

SCENE I
King Lear's palace.

Enter KENT, GLOUCESTER, *and* EDMUND

KENT I thought the King had more affected the Duke of Albany than Cornwall.

GLOUCESTER It did always seem so to us. But now in the division of the kingdom it appears not which of the Dukes he values most, for qualities are so weighed that care in neither can make choice of either's moiety.

KENT Is not this your son, my lord?

GLOUCESTER His breeding sir, has been at my charge. I have so often blushed to acknowledge him that now I am brazened to it.

KENT I cannot follow you.

GLOUCESTER Sir, this young fellow's mother could; whereupon she grew round-wombed, and had indeed, sir, a son for her cradle ere she had a husband for her bed. Do you smell a fault?

KENT I cannot wish the fault undone, the issue of it being so proper.

GLOUCESTER But I have a son, sir, by order of law, some year elder than this, who yet is no dearer in my account. Though this knave came something saucily to the world, before he was sent for, yet was his mother fair. There was good sport at his making, and the bastard must be acknowledged. Do you know this noble gentleman, Edmund?

EDMUND   No, my lord.

GLOUCESTER   My lord of Kent. Remember him
  hereafter as my honourable friend.

EDMUND   My services to your lordship.

KENT   I must love you and sue to know you better.

EDMUND   Sir, I shall study deserving.

GLOUCESTER   He has been out nine years, and away
  he shall again. The King is coming.

  Sound a sennet. Enter one bearing a coronet
  Enter King Lear, Cornwall, Albany, Goneril,
  Regan, Cordelia, and attendants

LEAR   Attend the lords of France and Burgundy,
  Gloucester.

GLOUCESTER   I shall, my liege.

  Exeunt Gloucester and Edmund

LEAR

  Meantime we shall express our darker purpose.
  Give me the map there. Know that we have divided
  In three our kingdom; it is our fast intent
  To shake all cares and business from our age,
  Conferring them on younger strengths, while we
  Unburdened crawl toward death. Our son of
    Cornwall—
  And you, our no less loving son of Albany—
  We have this hour a constant will to publish
  Our daughters' several dowers, that future strife
  May be prevented now. The princes, France and
    Burgundy,
  Great rivals in our youngest daughter's love,
  Long in our court have made their amorous sojourn,
  And here are to be answered. Tell me, my daughters,
  Since now we will divest us both of rule,
  Interest of territory, cares of state,
  Which of you shall we say does love us most,

That we our largest bounty may extend
Where nature does with merit challenge. Goneril,
Our eldest born, speak first.

GONERIL

Sir, I love you more than word can wield the matter,
Dearer than eyesight, space, and liberty,
Beyond what can be valued rich or rare,
No less than life, with grace, health, beauty, honour,
As much as child ever loved or father found;
A love that makes breath poor and speech unable.
Beyond all manner of 'so much' I love you.

CORDELIA *(aside)*

What shall Cordelia speak? Love, and be silent.

LEAR

Of all these bounds, even from this line to this,
With shadowy forests and with champains riched,
With plenteous rivers and wide-skirted meads,
We make you lady. To your and Albany's issues
Be this perpetual.—What says our second daughter,
Our dearest Regan, wife of Cornwall?

REGAN

I am made of that self mettle as my sister
And price me at her worth. In my true heart
I find she names my very deed of love;
Only she comes too short, that I profess
Myself an enemy to all other joys
Which the most precious square of sense possesses,
And find I am alone felicitate
In your dear highness' love.

CORDELIA *(aside)*   Then poor Cordelia!

And yet not so, since I am sure my love's
More ponderous than my tongue.

LEAR

To you and your hereditary ever
Remain this ample third of our fair kingdom,

No less in space, validity, and pleasure
Than that conferred on Goneril.—Now, our joy,
Although our last and least, to whose young love
The vines of France and milk of Burgundy
Strive for interest. What can you say to draw
A third more opulent than your sisters'? Speak!

CORDELIA   Nothing, my lord.

LEAR   Nothing?

CORDELIA   Nothing.

LEAR

Nothing will come of nothing. Speak again.

CORDELIA

Unhappy that I am, I cannot heave
My heart into my mouth. I love your majesty
According to my bond, no more nor less.

LEAR

How, how, Cordelia! Mend your speech a little
Lest you may mar your fortunes.

CORDELIA   Good my lord,
You have begot me, bred me, loved me.
I return those duties back as are right fit,
Obey you, love you, and most honour you.
Why have my sisters husbands, if they say
They love you all? Haply when I shall wed,
That lord whose hand must take my plight shall
   carry
Half my love with him, half my care and duty.
Sure I shall never marry like my sisters,
To love my father all.

LEAR

But goes your heart with this?

CORDELIA   Ay, my good lord.

LEAR   So young, and so untender?

CORDELIA   So young, my lord, and true.

LEAR
  Let it be so! Your truth then be your dower!
  For by the sacred radiance of the sun,
  The mysteries of Hecat and the night,
  By all the operation of the orbs
  From whom we do exist, and cease to be,
  Here I disclaim all my paternal care,
  Propinquity and property of blood,
  And as a stranger to my heart and me
  Hold you from this for ever. The barbarous Scythian,
  Or he that makes his progeny meals
  To gorge his appetite, shall to my bosom
  Be as well neighboured, pitied, and relieved
  As you my sometime daughter.

KENT   Good my liege—

LEAR Peace, Kent!
  Come not between the dragon and his wrath.
  I loved her most and thought to set my stake
  On her kind nursery. (*To Cordelia*) Hence and
    avoid my sight!—
  So be my grave my peace as here I give
  Her father's heart from her. Call France! Who stirs?
  Call Burgundy! Cornwall and Albany,
  With my two daughters' dowers digest the third.
  Let pride, which she calls plainness, marry her.
  I do invest you jointly with my power,
  Pre-eminence, and all the large effects
  That troop with majesty. Ourself by monthly course,
  With reservation of an hundred knights,
  By you to be sustained, shall our abode
  Make with you by due turn. Only we shall retain
  The name and all the addition to a king; the sway,
  Revènue, execution of the rest,

Beloved sons be yours; which to confirm,
This coronet part between you.

KENT   Royal Lear,
Whom I have ever honoured as my king,
Loved as my father, as my master followed,
As my great patron thought on in my prayers—

LEAR
The bow is bent and drawn; make from the shaft.

KENT
Let it fall rather, though the fork invades
The region of my heart. Be Kent unmannerly
When Lear is mad. What would you do, old man?
Think you that duty shall have dread to speak
When power to flattery bows? To plainness
    honour's bound
When majesty stoops to folly. Reserve your state,
And in your best consideration check
This hideous rashness. Answer my life my judgement,
Your youngest daughter does not love you least,
Nor are those empty-hearted whose low sounds
Reverb no hollowness.

LEAR   Kent, on your life, no more!

KENT
My life I never held but as a pawn
To wage against your enemies; nor fear to lose it,
Your safety being motive.

LEAR   Out of my sight!

KENT
See better, Lear, and let me still remain
The true aim of your eye.

LEAR
Now by Apollo—

KENT   Now by Apollo, King,

You swear your gods in vain.

LEAR   O vassal, miscreant!

ALBANY *and* CORNWALL   Dear sir, forbear!

KENT

Kill your physician and your fee bestow
Upon the foul disease. Revoke your gift,
Or while I can vent clamour from my throat
I'll tell you you do evil.

LEAR   Hear me, miscreant,
On your allegiance hear me!
That you have sought to make us break our vow,
Which we durst never yet and, with strained pride,
To come between our sentence and our power—
Which neither our nature nor our place can bear—
Our potency made good, take your reward.
Five days we do allot you for provision
To shield you from disasters of the world,
And on the sixth to turn your hated back
Upon our kingdom. If on the tenth day following
Your banished trunk is found in our dominions
The moment is your death. Away! By Jupiter,
This shall not be revoked!

KENT

Fare you well, King, since thus you will appear,
Freedom lives hence and banishment is here.
(To Cordelia)
The gods to their dear shelter take you, maid,
That justly think and have most rightly said.
(To Goneril and Regan)
And your large speeches may your deeds now prove
That good effects may spring from words of love.—
Thus Kent, O princes, bids you all adieu;
He'll shape his old course in a country new.   *Exit*

Flourish. Enter GLOUCESTER *with* KING OF
FRANCE, BURGUNDY, *and attendants*

GLOUCESTER
   Here are France, and Burgundy, my noble lord.
LEAR   My lord of Burgundy,
   We first address toward you, who with this king
   Has rivalled for our daughter: what in the least
   Will you require in present dower with her
   Or cease your quest of love?
BURGUNDY   Most royal majesty,
   I crave no more than has your highness offered,
   Nor will you tender less.
LEAR   Right noble Burgundy,
   When she was dear to us we did hold her so;
   But now her price is fallen. Sir, there she stands.
   If aught within that little-seeming substance,
   Or all of it, with our displeasure pieced,
   And nothing more, may fitly like your grace,
   She's there and she is yours.
BURGUNDY   I know no answer.
LEAR
   Will you with those infirmities she owns,
   Unfriended, new-adopted to our hate,
   Dowered with our curse and strangered with our
      oath,
   Take her or leave her?
BURGUNDY   Pardon me, royal sir,
   Election makes not up in such conditions.
LEAR
   Then leave her, sir, for, by the power that made me,
   I tell you all her wealth. (*To France*) For you, great
      king,
   I would not from your love make such a stray
   To match you where I hate. Therefore beseech you

To avert your liking a more worthy way
Than on a wretch whom Nature is ashamed
Almost to acknowledge hers.
FRANCE   This is most strange,
That she whom even but now was your best object,
The argument of your praise, balm of your age,
The best, the dearest, should in this trice of time
Commit a thing so monstrous to dismantle
So many folds of favour. Sure her offence
Must be of such unnatural degree
That monsters it; or your fore-said affection
Falls into taint. Which to believe of her
Must be a faith that reason without miracle
Should never plant in me.
CORDELIA   I yet beseech your majesty,
If, because I want that glib and oily art
To speak and purpose not, since what I well intend
I'll do it before I speak—that you make known
It is no vicious blot, murder or foulness,
No unchaste action or dishonoured step
That has deprived me of your grace and favour.
But even for want of that for which I am richer:
A still-soliciting eye and such a tongue
That I am glad I have not, though not to have it
Has lost me in your liking.
LEAR   Better you
Had not been born than not to have pleased me
    better.
FRANCE
Is it but this, a tardiness in nature
Which often leaves the history unspoken
That it intends to do? My lord of Burgundy,
What say you to the lady? Love's not love
When it is mingled with regards that stand
Aloof from the entire point. Will you have her?
She is herself a dowry.

BURGUNDY   Royal Lear,
  Give but that portion which yourself proposed
  And here I take Cordelia by the hand,
  Duchess of Burgundy.
LEAR
  Nothing! I have sworn; I am firm.
BURGUNDY   (*to Cordelia*)
  I am sorry then you have so lost a father
  That you must lose a husband.
CORDELIA   Peace be with Burgundy!
  Since then respect and fortunes are his love,
  I shall not be his wife.
KING OF FRANCE
  Fairest Cordelia, that are most rich, being poor,
  Most choice, forsaken, and most loved, despised,
  You and your virtues here I seize upon.
  Be it lawful I take up what's cast away.
  Gods, gods! 'Tis strange that from their cold neglect
  My love should kindle to inflamed respect.
  Your dowerless daughter, King, thrown to my
      chance,
  Is queen of us, of ours, and our fair France.
  Not all the dukes of waterish Burgundy
  Can buy this unprized-precious maid of me.
  Bid them farewell, Cordelia, though unkind.
  You now lose here, a better where to find.
LEAR
  You have her, France; let her be yours, for we
  Have no such daughter, nor shall ever see
  That face of hers again. Therefore begone,
  Without our grace, our love, our benison!
  Come, noble Burgundy.

        Flourish. Exeunt Lear, Burgundy, Cornwall,
        Albany, Gloucester, and attendants

KING OF FRANCE   Bid farewell to your sisters.

CORDELIA

The jewels of our father, with washèd eyes
Cordelia leaves you. I know you what you are;
And, like a sister, am most loth to call
Your faults as they are named. Love well our father!
To your professèd bosoms I commit him.
But yet, alas, stood I within his grace,
I would prefer him to a better place.
So farewell to you both.

REGAN

Prescribe not us our duty.

GONERIL   Let your study
Be to content your lord, who has received you
At Fortune's alms. You have obedience scanted,
And well are worth the want that you have wanted.

CORDELIA

Time shall unfold what plighted cunning hides;
Who covers faults, at last with shame derides.
Well may you prosper!

KING OF FRANCE   Come, my fair
Cordelia.

Exeunt King of France and Cordelia

GONERIL   Sister, it is not little I have to say of what
most nearly appertains to us both. I think our
father will hence tonight.

REGAN   That's most certain, and with you; next
month with us.

GONERIL   You see how full of changes his age is. The
observation we have made of it has not been little. He
always loved our sister most; and with what poor
judgement he has now cast her off appears too grossly.

REGAN   'Tis the infirmity of his age. Yet he has ever
but slenderly known himself.

GONERIL   The best and soundest of his time has been
but rash. Then must we look from his age to receive

not alone the imperfections of long-ingrafted
condition, but therewith the unruly waywardness
that infirm and choleric years bring with them.

REGAN   Such unconstant starts are we like to have from
him as this of Kent's banishment.

GONERIL   There is further compliment of leave-taking
between France and him. Pray you, let us hit together.
If our father carries authority with such disposition as
he bears, this last surrender of his will but offend us.

REGAN   We shall further think of it.

GONERIL   We must do something, and in the heat.

Exeunt

SCENE II
Gloucester's castle.

Enter EDMUND, *with a letter*

EDMUND

You, Nature are my goddess; to your law
My services are bound. Wherefore should I
Stand in the plague of custom and permit
The curiosity of nations to deprive me,
Because I am some twelve or fourteen moonshines
Behind a brother? Why bastard? Wherefore base?
When my dimensions are as well-compact,
My mind as generous, and my shape as true
As honest madam's issue? Why brand they us
With 'base'? with 'baseness'? 'bastardy'? 'base, base'?
Who in the lusty stealth of nature take
More composition and fierce quality
Than does within a dull, stale, tirèd bed
Go to the creating a whole tribe of fops
Go between asleep and wake? Well then,
Legitimate Edgar, I must have your land.

Our father's love is to the bastard Edmund
As to the legitimate. Fine word 'legitimate'!
Well, my 'legitimate', if this letter speeds
And my invention thrives, Edmund the base
Shall top the legitimate. I grow. I prosper.
Now gods stand up for bastards!

Enter GLOUCESTER

GLOUCESTER
Kent banished thus? and France in choler parted?
And the King gone tonight? prescribed his power?
Confined to maintenance? All this done
On a sudden? Edmund, how now? What news?

EDMUND   So please your lordship, none.

GLOUCESTER   Why so earnestly seek you to put up
that letter?

EDMUND   I know no news, my lord.

GLOUCESTER   What paper were you reading?

EDMUND   Nothing, my lord.

GLOUCESTER   No? What needed then that terrible
dispatch of it into your pocket? The quality of
nothing has not such need to hide itself. Let's see!
Come! If it is nothing I shall not need spectacles.

EDMUND   I beseech you, sir, pardon me. It is a letter
from my brother that I have not all over-read; and for
so much as I have perused, I find it not fit for your
overlooking.

GLOUCESTER   Give me the letter, sir.

EDMUND   I shall offend either to detain or give it. The
contents, as in part I understand them, are to blame.

GLOUCESTER   Let's see, let's see!

EDMUND   I hope for my brother's justification he wrote
this but as an essay or taste of my virtue.

GLOUCESTER   (*reading*) *This policy and reverence of age
make the world bitter to the best of our times,*

keep our fortunes from us till our oldness cannot
relish them. I begin to find an idle and fond
bondage in the oppression of agèd tyranny, who
sways not as it has power but as it is suffered.
Come to me that of this I may speak more. If our
father would sleep till I waked him, you should
enjoy half his revenue for ever, and live the beloved
of your brother,

> *Edgar.*

Hum! Conspiracy! 'Sleep till I waked him, you
should enjoy half his revenue'. My son Edgar, had
he a hand to write this? a heart and brain to breed
it in? When came you to this? Who brought it?

EDMUND   It was not brought me, my lord. There's
the cunning of it. I found it thrown in at the
casement of my closet.

GLOUCESTER   You know the character to be your
brother's?

EDMUND   If the matter was good, my lord, I durst
swear it was his; but in respect of that I would
fain think it was not.

GLOUCESTER   It is his!

EDMUND   It is his hand, my lord; but I hope his heart
is not in the contents.

GLOUCESTER   Has he never before sounded you in
this business?

EDMUND   Never, my lord. But I have heard him
oft maintain it to be fit that, sons at perfect age and
fathers declined, the father should be as ward to the
son, and the son manage his revenue.

GLOUCESTER   O villain, villain! His very opinion
in the letter! Abhorred villain! Unnatural, detested,
brutish villian! worse than brutish! Go, sir, seek
him. I'll apprehend him. Abominable villain!
Where is he?

EDMUND   I do not well know, my lord. If it shall
please you to suspend your indignation against my
brother till you can derive from him better
testimony of his intent, you should run a certain
course. Where, if you violently proceed against
him, mistaking his purpose, it would make a great
gap in your own honour and shake in pieces the
heart of his obedience. I dare pawn down my life
for him that he has written this to feel my affection
to your honour and to no other pretence of danger.

GLOUCESTER   Think you so?

EDMUND   If your honour judges it meet I will place
you where you shall hear us confer of this and by
an auricular assurance have your satisfaction, and
that without any further delay than this very evening.

GLOUCESTER   He cannot be such a monster—

EDMUND   And is not, sure.

GLOUCESTER   To his father that so tenderly and
entirely loves him. Heaven and earth! Edmund,
seek him out. Wind me into him, I pray you.
Frame the business after your own wisdom. I
would unstate myself to be in a due resolution.

EDMUND   I will seek him, sir, at once, convey the
business as I shall find means, and acquaint you
with it.

GLOUCESTER   These late eclipses in the sun and moon
portend no good to us. Though the wisdom of
nature can reason it thus and thus, yet nature finds
itself scourged by the sequent effects: love cools,
friendship falls off, brothers divide. In cities,
mutinies; in countries, discord; in palaces, treason;
and the bond cracked between son and father. This
villain of mine comes under the prediction: there's
son against father; the King falls from bias of
nature: there's father against child. We have seen

the best of our time. Machinations, hollowness,
treachery, and all ruinous disorders follow us
disquietly to our graves. Find out this villain,
Edmund; it shall lose you nothing; do it carefully—
and the noble and true-hearted Kent banished! His
offence, honesty! 'Tis strange.　　　　　　　　　*Exit*

EDMUND　This is the excellent foppery of the world
that, when we are sick in fortune—often the
surfeits of our own behaviour—we make guilty of
our disasters the sun, the moon, and stars. As if we
were villains on necessity, fools by heavenly
compulsion; knaves, thieves, and traitors by
spherical predominance; drunkards, liars, and
adulterers by an enforced obedience of planetary
influence; and all that we are evil in by a divine
thrusting-on. An admirable evasion of whoremaster
man to lay his goatish disposition to the charge of a
star. My father compounded with my mother under
the Dragon's tail, and my nativity was under Ursa
Major, so that it follows I am rough and lecherous.
Fut! I should have been that I am had the
maidenliest star in the firmament twinkled on my
bastardizing. Edgar—

(*Enter* EDGAR)

pat he comes, like the catastrophe of the old
comedy. My cue is villainous melancholy, with a
sigh like Tom o'Bedlam. (*Aloud*) O these eclipses
do portend these divisions: (*he sings*) Fa, sol, la, mi.

EDGAR　How now, brother Edmund! What serious
contemplation are you in?

EDMUND　I am thinking, brother, of a prediction I read
this other day, what should follow these eclipses.

EDGAR　Do you busy yourself with that?

EDMUND I promise you, the effects he writes of
succeed unhappily, as of unnaturalness between the
child and the parent; death, dearth, dissolutions of
ancient amities; divisions in state, menaces and
maledictions against king and nobles; needless
mistrusts, banishment of friends, dissipation of
cohorts, nuptial breaches, and I know not what.

EDGAR How long have you been a disciple
astronomical?

EDMUND When saw you my father last?

EDGAR The night gone by.

EDMUND Spoke you with him?

EDGAR Ay, two hours together.

EDMUND Parted you in good terms? Found you no
displeasure in him by word or countenance?

EDGAR None at all.

EDMUND Bethink yourself wherein you may have
offended him, and at my entreaty forbear his
presence until some little time has qualified the
heat of his displeasure. Which at this instant so
rages in him that with the mischief of your person
it would scarcely abate.

EDGAR Some villain has done me wrong.

EDMUND That's my fear. I pray you have a continent
forbearance till the speed of his rage goes slower;
and, as I say, retire with me to my lodging, from
whence I will fitly bring you to hear my lord speak.
Pray you, go! There's my key. If you do stir abroad,
go armed.

EDGAR Armed, brother?

EDMUND Brother, I advise you to the best. I am no
honest man if there is any good meaning toward
you. I have told you what I have seen and heard but
faintly, nothing like the image and horror of it.
Pray you, away!

EDGAR   Shall I hear from you anon?
EDMUND   I do serve you in this business.

                                                              Exit Edgar

   A credulous father and a brother noble,
   Whose nature is so far from doing harms
   That he suspects none; on whose foolish honesty
   My practices ride easy. I see the business:
   Let me, if not by birth, have lands by wit;
   All with me's meet that I can fashion fit.   *Exit*

SCENE III
Albany's palace.

Enter GONERIL *and* OSWALD, *her steward*

GONERIL   Did my father strike my gentleman for
  chiding of his Fool?
OSWALD   Ay, Madam.
GONERIL
   By day and night he wrongs me; every hour
   He flashes into one gross crime or other
   That sets us all at odds. I'll not endure it!
   His knights grow riotous, and himself upbraids us
   On every trifle. When he returns from hunting
   I will not speak with him. Say I am sick.
   If you come slack of former services
   You shall do well; the fault of it I'll answer.
OSWALD   He's coming, madam; I hear him.
GONERIL
   Put on what weary negligence you please,
   You and your fellows. I'd have it come to question.
   If he distastes it let him to my sister,
   Whose mind and mine I know in that are one,
   Not to be overruled. Idle old man,

That still would manage those authorities
That he has given away! Now, by my life,
Old fools are babes again, and must be used
With checks as flatteries, when they are seen
   abused.
Remember what I have said.

OSWALD   Well, madam.

GONERIL

And let his knights have colder looks among you.
What grows of it, no matter. Advise your fellows so.
I would breed from hence occasions, and I shall,
That I may speak. I'll write straight to my sister
To hold my very course. Prepare for dinner.   *Exeunt*

SCENE IV
The same.

Enter KENT *in disguise*

KENT

If but as well I other accents borrow
That can my speech diffuse, my good intent
May carry through itself to that full issue
For which I changed my likeness. Now, banished
   Kent,
If you can serve where you do stand condemned,
So may it come your master whom you love
Shall find you full of labours.

Horns within. Enter LEAR *and* KNIGHTS

LEAR   Let me not stay a jot for dinner! Go, get it
ready!

                           Exit First Knight

How now? What are you?

KENT   A man, sir.

LEAR   What do you profess? What would you with us?

KENT   I do profess to be no less than I seem: to serve
him truly that will put me in trust, to love him
that is honest, to converse with him that is wise
and says little, to fear judgement, to fight when I
cannot choose, and to eat no fish.

LEAR   What are you?

KENT   A very honest-hearted fellow, and as poor as
the King.

LEAR   If you are as poor for a subject as he is for a
king you are poor enough. What would you?

KENT   Service.

LEAR   Whom would you serve?

KENT   You.

LEAR   Do you know me, fellow?

KENT   No, sir; but you have that in your countenance
which I would fain call master.

LEAR   What's that?

KENT   Authority.

LEAR   What services can you do?

KENT   I can keep honest counsel, ride, run, mar a
strange tale in telling it, and deliver a plain message
bluntly. That which ordinary men are fit for I am
qualified in, and the best of me is diligence.

LEAR   How old are you?

KENT   Not so young, sir, to love a woman for singing,
nor so old to dote on her for anything. I have years
on my back forty-eight.

LEAR   Follow me; you shall serve me if I like you no
worse after dinner. I will not part from you yet.
Dinner, ho, dinner! Where's my knave, my Fool?
Go you and call my Fool hither. *Exit Second Knight*

Enter OSWALD

You! You, fellow! Where's my daughter?
OSWALD   So please you—   *Exit*
LEAR   What says the fellow there? Call the blockhead
   back.   *Exit Third Knight*
   Where's my Fool? Ho, I think the world's asleep.

Enter THIRD KNIGHT

How now? Where's that mongrel?
THIRD KNIGHT   He says, my lord, your daughter is not
   well.
LEAR   Why came not the slave back to me when I
   called him?
THIRD KNIGHT   Sir, he answered me in the roundest
   manner he would not.
LEAR   He would not!
THIRD KNIGHT   My lord, I know not what the matter
   is, but to my judgement your highness is not
   entertained with that ceremonious affection as you
   were wont. There's a great abatement of kindness
   appears as well in the general dependants as in the
   Duke himself also and your daughter.
LEAR   Ha! Say you so?
THIRD KNIGHT   I beseech you pardon me, my lord, if I
   am mistaken; for my duty cannot be silent when I
   think your highness wronged.
LEAR   You but remember me of my own impression.
   I have perceived a most faint neglect of late,
   which I have rather blamed as my own jealous
   fancy than as a very pretence and purpose of

unkindness. I will look further into it. But where's
my Fool? I have not seen him these two days.

THIRD KNIGHT   Since my young lady's going into
France, sir, the Fool has much pined away.

LEAR   No more of that! I have noted it well. Go you
and tell my daughter I would speak with her.

Exit Third Knight

Go you, call hither my Fool.   *Exit another Knight*

Enter OSWALD

O, you, sir, you! Come you hither, sir. Who am I,
sir?

OSWALD   My lady's father.

LEAR   'My lady's father', my lord's knave! You dog!
You slave! You cur!

OSWALD   I am none of these, my lord, I beseech your
pardon.

LEAR   Do you bandy looks with me, you rascal?

He strikes him

OSWALD   I'll not be struck, my lord.

KENT   Nor tripped either, you base football-player?

He trips him

LEAR   I thank you, fellow. You serve me and I'll love
you.

KENT   *(to Oswald)* Come, sir, arise, away! I'll teach you
differences. Away, away! If you will measure your
lubber's length again, tarry; but away, go to! Have
you wisdom?

He pushes OSWALD *out*

So.

LEAR Now, my friendly knave, I thank you. There's
earnest of your service.

He gives him money
Enter the FOOL

FOOL Let me hire him too. Here's my coxcomb.

LEAR How now, my pretty knave! How do you?

FOOL Fellow, you were best take my coxcomb.

KENT Why, Fool?

FOOL Why? For taking one's part that's out of favour.
Nay, if you can not smile as the wind sits, you'll
catch cold shortly. There, take my coxcomb! Why,
this fellow has banished two of his daughters, and
did the third a blessing against his will. If you
follow him, you must needs wear my coxcomb.
How now, uncle! Would I had two coxcombs and
two daughters!

LEAR Why, my boy?

FOOL If I gave them all my living, I'd keep my
coxcombs myself. There's mine. Beg another of
your daughters.

LEAR Take heed, fellow, the whip!

FOOL Truth's a dog must to kennel; he must be
whipped out when the Lady Bitch-hound may stand
by the fire and stink.

LEAR A pestilent gall to me!

FOOL Sir, I'll teach you a speech.

LEAR Do.

FOOL Mark it, uncle:
    Have more than you show,
    Speak less than you know,
    Lend less than you owe,
    Ride more than you go [walk],

Learn more than you know,
Stake less than you throw,
Leave your drink and your whore
And keep in-at-door,
And you shall have more
Than two tens to a score.

KENT   This is nothing, Fool.

FOOL   Then it is like the breath of an unfeed lawyer:
you gave me nothing for it. Can you make no use
of nothing, uncle?

LEAR   Why, no, boy. Nothing can be made out of
nothing.

FOOL   (*to Kent*) Pray tell him; so much the rent of
his land comes to. He will not believe a fool.

LEAR   A bitter fool!

FOOL   Do you know the difference, my boy, between
a bitter fool and a sweet one?

LEAR   No, lad; teach me.

FOOL

That lord that counselled you
    To give away your land,
Come place him here by me;
    Do you for him stand.
The sweet and bitter fool
    Will presently appear:
The one in motley here,
    The other found out—there.

LEAR   Do you call me fool, boy?

FOOL   All your other titles you have given away; that
you were born with.

KENT   This is not altogether fool, my lord.

FOOL   No, faith; lords and great men will not stop
me. If I had a monopoly out they would have part
of it; and ladies too—they will not let me have all the

fool to myself; they'll be snatching. Uncle, give
me an egg and I'll give you two crowns.

LEAR   What two crowns shall they be?

FOOL   Why, after I have cut the egg in the middle
and eaten up the meat, the two crowns of the egg.
When you clove your crown in the middle, and
gave away both parts, you bore your ass on your
back over the dirt. You had little wit in your bald
crown when you gave your golden one away. If I
speak like myself in this, let him be whipped that
first finds it so.

   Fools had never less grace in a year,
     For wise men are grown foppish,
   And know not how their wits to wear,
     Their manners are so apish.

LEAR   When were you wont to be so full of songs,
boy?

FOOL   I have used it, uncle, ever since you made
your daughters your mothers; for when you gave
them the rod and put down your own breeches,

(sings)

   Then they for sudden joy did weep,
     And I for sorrow sung,
   That such a king should play bo-peep
     And go the fools among.

Pray, uncle, keep a schoolmaster that can teach
your fool to lie; I would fain learn to lie.

LEAR   If you lie, we'll have you whipped.

FOOL   I marvel what kin you and your daughters are.
They'll have me whipped for speaking true; you'll
have me whipped for lying; and sometimes I am
whipped for holding my peace. I had rather be any

kind of thing than a fool. And yet I would not be
you, uncle. You have pared your wit on both sides
and left nothing in the middle. Here comes one
of the parings.

Enter GONERIL

LEAR   How now, daughter! Why put on that frown?
  You are too much of late in the frown.
FOOL   You were a pretty fellow when you had no
  need to care for her frowning. Now you are an 0
  without a figure. I am better than you are now; I
  am a fool; you are nothing. *(To Goneril)* Yes,
  indeed, I will hold my tongue. So your face bids
  me, though you say nothing.
    Mum, mum!
    He that keeps nor crust nor crumb,
    Weary of all, shall want some.

He points to LEAR

  That's a shelled peascod.
GONERIL
  Not only, sir, this your all-licensed fool
  But others of your insolent retinue
  Do hourly carp and quarrel, breaking forth
  In rank and not-to-be endurèd riots. Sir,
  I had thought by making this well known unto you
  To have found a safe redress. But now grow fearful
  By what yourself too late have spoken and done
  That you protect this course and put it on
  By your allowance. Which if you should, the fault
  Would not escape censure, nor the redresses sleep;
  Which in the tender of a wholesome weal
  Might in their working do you that offence,

Which else were shame, that then necessity
Will call discreet proceeding

FOOL   For you know, uncle,
The hedge-sparrow fed the cuckoo so long
That it had its head bit off by its young.
So out went the candle and we were left darkling.

LEAR   Are you our daughter?

GONERIL
I would you would make use of your good wisdom,
Whereof I know you are stored, and put away
These dispositions which of late transport you
From what you rightly are.

FOOL   May not an ass know when the cart draws
the horse?
Whoop, Jug, I love you!

LEAR
Does any here know me? This is not Lear.
Does Lear walk thus, speak thus? Where are his
eyes?
Either his notion weakens, his discernings
Are lethargied—Ha! Waking? 'Tis not so!
Who is it that can tell me who I am?

FOOL   Lear's shadow.

LEAR   I would learn that; for by the marks of
sovereignty, knowledge, and reason, I should be
false persuaded I had daughters.

FOOL   Which they will make an obedient father.

LEAR   Your name, fair gentlewoman?

GONERIL
This wonderment, sir, is much of the savour
Of others of your new pranks. I do beseech you
To understand my purposes aright:
As you are old and reverend, should be wise.
Here do you keep a hundred knights and squires,
Men so disordered, so debauched and bold,

That this our court, infected with their manners,
Shows like a riotous inn. Epicurism and lust
Make it more like a tavern or a brothel
Than a graced palace. The shame itself does speak
For instant remedy. Be then desired,
By her that else will take the thing she begs,
A little to disquantity your train;
And the remainders that shall still depend
To be such men as may besort your age,
Who know themselves and you.

LEAR   Darkness and devils!
Saddle my horses! Call my train together!
Degenerate bastard, I'll not trouble you.
Yet have I left a daughter.

GONERIL

You strike my people, and your disordered rabble
Make servants of their betters.

Enter ALBANY

LEAR

Woe that too late repents!—O, sir, are you come?
Is it your will? Speak, sir!—Prepare my horses.
Ingratitude, you marble-hearted fiend,
More hideous when you show up in a child
Than the sea-monster!

ALBANY   Pray, sir, be patient.

LEAR *(to Goneril)*

Detested kite, you lie!
My train are men of choice and rarest parts,
That all particulars of duty know
And in the most exact regard support
The worships of their name. O most small fault,
How ugly did you in Cordelia show!
Which, like an engine, wrenched my frame of nature

From the fixed place, drew from my heart all love,
And added to the gall. O Lear, Lear, Lear!
Beat at this gate that let your folly in

(he strikes his head)

And your dear judgement out! Go, go, my people.
                              Exeunt Kent and Knights

ALBANY
My lord, I am guiltless as I am ignorant
Of what has moved you.

LEAR   It may be so, my lord.

He kneels

Hear, Nature, hear! Dear goddess, hear!
Suspend your purpose if you did intend
To make this creature fruitful.
Into her womb convey sterility,
Dry up in her the organs of increase,
And from her derogate body never spring
A babe to honour her. If she must breed,
Create her child of evil, that it may live
And be a thwart disnatured torment to her.
Let it stamp wrinkles in her brow of youth,
With cadent tears fret channels in her cheeks,
Turn all her mother's pains and benefits
To laughter and contempt—that she may feel
How sharper than a serpent's tooth it is
To have a thankless child! Away, away!   *Exit*

ALBANY
Now gods that we adore, whereof comes this?

GONERIL
Never afflict yourself to know more of it;

But let his disposition have that scope
As dotage gives it.

Enter LEAR

LEAR
What, fifty of my followers at a clap?
Within a fortnight?
ALBANY   What's the matter, sir?
LEAR
I'll tell you—(*to Goneril*) life and death! I am
   ashamed
That you have power to shake my manhood thus,
That these hot tears which break from me perforce
Should make you worth them. Blasts and fogs upon
   you!
The unprobed woundings of a father's curse
Pierce every sense about you!—Old foolish eyes,
Beweep this cause again, I'll pluck you out
And cast you with the waters that you loose
To temper clay. Yea, is it come to this?
Let it be so. I have another daughter,
Who, I am sure, is kind and comfortable.
When she shall hear this of you, with her nails
She'll flay your wolvish visage. You shall find
That I'll resume the shape which you do think
I have cast off for ever.   *Exit*
GONERIL   Do you mark that?
ALBANY
I cannot be so partial, Goneril,
To the great love I bear you—
GONERIL
Pray you, content—What, Oswald, ho!
(*To the Fool*) You, sir, more knave than fool, after
   your master!

FOOL   Uncle Lear, uncle Lear, tarry! Take the Fool
  with you.

> A fox, when one has caught her,
> And such a daughter
> Should sure to the slaughter,
> If my cap would buy a halter—
> So the fool follows after.   *Exit*

GONERIL

  This man has had good counsel! A hundred knights!
  'Tis politic and safe to let him keep
  In action a hundred knights! Yes, that on every dream,
  Each buzz, each fancy, each complaint, dislike,
  He may enguard his dotage with their powers
  And hold our lives in mercy.—Oswald, I say!

ALBANY

  Well, you may fear too far.

GONERIL   Safer than trust too far.

  Let me ever take away the harms I fear,
  Not fear ever to be taken. I know his heart.
  What he has uttered I have written my sister;
  If she sustains him and his hundred knights
  When I have showed the unfitness—

Enter OSWALD

                              How now, Oswald!

  What, have you written that letter to my sister?

OSWALD   Ay, madam.

GONERIL

  Take you some company and away to horse.
  Inform her full of my particular fear,
  And thereto add such reasons of your own
  As may compact it more. Get you gone,
  And hasten your return.   *Exit Oswald*

                      No, no, my lord,

This milky gentleness and course of yours,
Though I condemn not, yet, under pardon,
You are much more a-taxed for want of wisdom
Than praised for harmful mildness.

ALBANY

How far your eyes may pierce I cannot tell;
Striving to better, oft we mar what's well.

GONERIL   Nay then—

ALBANY   Well, well—the event!   *Exeunt*

SCENE V
Before Albany's palace.

Enter LEAR, KENT, KNIGHT, *and the* FOOL

LEAR   *(to Kent)* Go you before to Gloucester with
these letters. Acquaint my daughter no further with
anything you know than comes from her demand
out of the letter. If your diligence is not speedy I
shall be there before you.

KENT   I will not sleep, my lord, till I have delivered
your letter.   *Exit*

FOOL   If a man's brains were in his heels, were it not
in danger of chilblains?

LEAR   Ay, boy.

FOOL   Then I pray you be merry. Your wit shall not
go slipshod.

LEAR   Ha, ha, ha!

FOOL   You shall see your other daughter will use you
kindly; for though she's as like this as a crab's
like an apple, yet I can tell what I can tell.

LEAR   What can you tell, boy?

FOOL   She will taste as like this as a crab does to a
crab.

You can tell why one's nose stands in the middle
of his face?

LEAR   No.

FOOL   Why, to keep one's eyes on either side of his
nose; that what a man cannot smell out he may
spy into.

LEAR   I did her wrong.

FOOL   Can you tell how an oyster makes his shell?

LEAR   No.

FOOL   Nor I either. But I can tell why a snail has a
house.

LEAR   Why?

FOOL   Why, to put his head in; not to give it away to
his daughters, and leave his horns without a case.

LEAR   I will forget my nature. So kind a father!—Are
my horses ready?

FOOL   Your asses are gone about them. The reason
why the seven stars are no more than seven is a
pretty reason.

LEAR   Because they are not eight?

FOOL   Yes, indeed. You would make a good fool.

LEAR   To take it again perforce! Monster ingratitude!

FOOL   If you were my fool, uncle, I'd have you beaten
for being old before your time.

LEAR   How's that?

FOOL   You should not have been old till you had
been wise.

LEAR

O let me not be mad, not mad, sweet heaven!
Keep me in temper; I would not be mad!
How now! Are the horses ready?

KNIGHT   Ready, my lord.

LEAR   Come, boy.   *Exeunt all except the Fool*

FOOL

She that's a maid now, and laughs at my departure,
Shall not be a maid long, unless things are cut shorter.
                                                   Exit

Act II

SCENE I
Before Gloucester's castle.

Enter EDMUND *and* CURAN *by opposite doors*

EDMUND Save you, Curan.

CURAN And you, sir. I have been with your father
and given him notice that the Duke of Cornwall
and Regan his Duchess will be here with him
this night.

EDMUND How comes that?

CURAN Nay, I know not. You have heard of the news
abroad—I mean the whispered ones, for they are
yet but ear-kissing arguments?

EDMUND Not I. Pray you what are they?

CURAN Have you heard of no likely wars toward
between the Dukes of Cornwall and Albany?

EDMUND Not a word.

CURAN You may do, then, in time. Fare you well,
sir.   *Exit*

EDMUND

The Duke be here tonight! The better! best!
This weaves itself perforce into my business.
My father has set guard to take my brother,
And I have one thing of a queasy question
Which I must act. Briefness and fortune work!—
Brother, a word! Descend! Brother, I say!

Enter EDGAR

My father watches. O, sir, fly this place;
Intelligence is given where you are hidden.

You have now the good advantage of the night.
Have you not spoken against the Duke of Cornwall?
He's coming hither now in the night, in haste,
And Regan with him. Have you nothing said
Upon his part against the Duke of Albany?
Advise yourself.

EDGAR   I am sure of it, not a word.

EDMUND

I hear my father coming. Pardon me;
In cunning I must draw my sword upon you.
Draw! Seem to defend yourself! Now quit you well.
(*Aloud*) Yield! Come before my father! Light, ho,
   here!
(*Aside*) Fly, brother! (*Aloud*) Torches, torches!
   (*Aside*) So farewell.   *Exit Edgar*
Some blood drawn on me would beget opinion
Of my more fierce endeavour. I have seen drunkards
Do more than this in sport.

> *He stabs himself in the arm*

                 (*Aloud*) Father, father!—
Stop, stop!—No help?

> *Enter* GLOUCESTER *and servants with torches*

GLOUCESTER   Now, Edmund, where's the
   villain?

EDMUND

Here stood he in the dark, his sharp sword out,
Mumbling of wicked charms, conjuring the moon
To stand auspicious mistress.

GLOUCESTER   But where is he?

EDMUND

Look, sir, I bleed.

GLOUCESTER   Where is the villain, Edmund?

EDMUND

  Fled this way, sir, when by no means he could—
GLOUCESTER

  Pursue him, ho! Go after.   *Exeunt servants*
                              'By no means' what?

EDMUND

  Persuade me to the murder of your lordship;
  But that I told him the revenging gods
  Against parricides did all the thunder bend,
  Spoke with how manifold and strong a bond
  The child was bound to the father. Sir, in fine,
  Seeing how loathly opposite I stood
  To his unnatural purpose, in fierce motion
  With his preparèd sword he charges home
  My unprovided body, latched my arm.
  But when he saw my best alarumed spirits
  Bold in the quarrel's right, roused to the encounter,
  Or whether frightened by the noise I made,
  Full suddenly he fled.

GLOUCESTER   Let him fly far,
  Not in this land shall he remain uncaught;
  And found—dispatch. The noble Duke, my master,
  My worthy arch and patron, comes tonight.
  By his authority I will proclaim it
  That he who finds him shall deserve our thanks,
  Bringing the murderous coward to the stake;
  He that conceals him, death.

EDMUND

  When I dissuaded him from his intent,
  And found him fixed to do it, with cursed speech
  I threatened to discover him. He replied,
  'You unpossessing bastard, do you think,
  If I would stand against you, would the reposal
  Of any trust, virtue, or worth in you
  Make your words faithed? No, what I should deny—

As this I would; ay, though you did produce
My very character—I'd turn it all
To your suggestion, plot, and damnèd practice.
And you must make a dullard of the world
If they not thought the profits of my death
Were very pregnant and potential spirits
To make you seek it.'
GLOUCESTER   O strange, determined villain!
Would he deny his letter, said he? I never begot him.

Tucket within

Hark, the Duke's trumpets! I know not why he
    comes.—
All gates I'll bar; the villain shall not escape.
The Duke must grant me that. Besides, his picture
I will send far and near, that all the kingdom
May have due note of him; and of my land,
Loyal and natural boy, I'll work the means
To make you heir.

Enter CORNWALL, REGAN, *and attendants*

CORNWALL
How now, my noble friend? Since I came hither—
Which I can call but now—I have heard strange
    news.
REGAN
If it is true, all vengeance comes too short
Which can pursue the offender. How do you,
    my lord?
GLOUCESTER
O madam, my old heart is cracked; it's cracked.
REGAN
What, did my father's godson seek your life?

He whom my father named? your Edgar?
GLOUCESTER
O lady, lady, shame would have it hidden.
REGAN
Was he not companion with the riotous knights
That attended on my father?
GLOUCESTER
I know not, madam, 'Tis too bad, too bad!
EDMUND
Yes, madam, he was of that consòrt.
REGAN
No marvel then that he was ill affected.
'Tis they have put him on the old man's death,
To have the expense and waste of his revènues.
I have this present evening from my sister
Been well informed of them, and with such cautions
That if they come to sojourn at my house
I'll not be there.
CORNWALL   Nor I, assure you, Regan.
Edmund, I hear that you have shown your father
A child-like office.
EDMUND   It was my duty, sir.
GLOUCESTER
He did reveal his malice, and received
This hurt you see, striving to apprehend him.
CORNWALL
Is he pursued?
GLOUCESTER   Ay, my good lord.
CORNWALL
If he is taken he shall never more
Be feared of doing harm. Make your own purpose
How in my strength you please. For you, Edmund,
Whose virtue and obedience do this instant
So much commend itself, you shall be ours.
Natures of such deep trust we shall much need;
You we first seize on.

EDMUND   I shall serve you, sir,
  Truly, however else.
GLOUCESTER   For him I thank your grace.
CORNWALL
  You know not why we came to visit you—
REGAN
  Thus out of season, threading dark-eyed night—
  Occasions, noble Gloucester, of some price,
  Wherein we must have use of your advice.
  Our father he has written, so has our sister,
  Of differences, which I best thought it fit
  To answer from our home. The several messengers
  From hence attend dispatch. Our good old friend,
  Lay comforts to your bosom, and bestow
  Your needful counsel to our businesses,
  Which crave the instant use.
GLOUCESTER   I serve you, madam.
  Your graces are right welcome.   *Exeunt. Flourish*

SCENE II
The same.

Enter KENT *and* OSWALD *by opposite doors*

OSWALD
  Good dawning to you, friend. Are you of this house?
KENT   Ay.
OSWALD   Where may we set our horses?
KENT   In the mire.
OSWALD   Pray, if you love me, tell me.
KENT   I love you not.
OSWALD   Why then, I care not for you.
KENT   If I had you between my teeth I would make you
  care for me.
OSWALD   Why do you use me thus? I know you not.

KENT   Fellow, I know you.

OSWALD   What do you know me for?

KENT   A knave, a rascal, an eater of scraps, a base,
proud, shallow, beggarly, three-suited, hundred-
pound, filthy-worsted-stocking knave; a lily-livered,
action-taking, glass-gazing super-serviceable finical
rogue, one-trunk-inheriting slave. One that would be
a bawd in way of good service, and are nothing but
the compound of a knave, beggar, coward, pander,
and the son and heir of a mongrel bitch. One whom
I will beat into clamorous whining if you deny the
least syllable of your description.

OSWALD   Why, what a monstrous fellow are you thus
to rail on one that is neither known by you nor
knows you!

KENT   What a brazen-faced varlet are you, to deny you
know me! Is it two days since I tripped up your heels
and beat you before the King? Draw, you rogue! For
though it is night, yet the moon shines. I'll make a
sop of the moonshine of you, you base barber-
monger! Draw!

He draws his sword

OSWALD   Away! I have nothing to do with you.

KENT   Draw, you rascal! You come with letters against
the King, and take Vanity the puppet's part against
the royalty of her father. Draw, you rogue! or I'll so
slash your shanks—Draw, you rascal! Come your
ways!

OSWALD   Help, ho! Murder! Help!

KENT   Strike, you slave!
Stand, rogue! Stand, you neat slave! Strike!

He beats him

OSWALD   Help, ho! Murder! Murder!

Enter EDMUND, CORNWALL, REGAN, GLOUCESTER,
and servants

EDMUND   How now! What's the matter? Part!
KENT   With you, goodman boy, and you please!
   Come, I'll flesh you; come on, young master.
GLOUCESTER   Weapons? Arms? What's the matter here?
CORNWALL
   Keep peace, upon your lives!
   He dies that strikes again. What is the matter?
REGAN
   The messengers from our sister and the King—
CORNWALL   What is your difference? Speak.
OSWALD   I am scarce in breath, my lord.
KENT   No marvel, you have so bestirred your valour.
   You cowardly rascal, nature disclaims in you; a
   tailor made you.
CORNWALL   You are a strange fellow. A tailor make a
   man?
KENT   A tailor, sir. A stone-cutter or a painter could
   not have made him so ill, though they had been
   but two years in the trade.
CORNWALL   *(to Oswald)* Speak yet, how grew your
   quarrel?
OSWALD   This ancient ruffian, sir, whose life I have
   spared at suit of his grey beard—
KENT   You bastardly zed, you unnecessary letter! My
   lord, if you will give me leave, I will tread this
   unsifted villain into mortar and daub the wall of a
   jakes with him. 'Spare my grey beard', you wagtail!
CORNWALL   Peace, fellow!
   You beastly knave, know you no reverence?
KENT
   Yes, sir; but anger has a privilege.

CORNWALL   Why are you angry?
KENT

That such a slave as this should wear a sword
Who wears no honesty. Such smiling rogues as
    these,
Like rats, oft bite the holy cords in two—
Too inward to unloose; smooth every passion
That in the natures of their lords rebel,
Bring oil to fire, snow to the colder moods;
Renege, affirm, and turn their halcyon beaks
With every gale and vary of their masters,
Knowing naught—like dogs—but following.—
A plague upon your epileptic visage—
Smile at my speeches as I were a fool?
Goose, if I had you upon Sarum Plain,
I'd drive you cackling home to Camelot.
CORNWALL   What, are you mad, old fellow?
GLOUCESTER   How fell you out? Say that.
KENT

No contraries hold more antipathy
Than I and such a knave.

CORNWALL

Why do you call him knave? What is his fault?
KENT   His countenance likes me not.
CORNWALL

No more perchance does mine, nor his, nor hers.
KENT

Sir, 'tis my occupation to be plain.
I have seen better faces in my time
Than stands on any shoulder that I see
Before me at this instant.
CORNWALL   This is some fellow
Who, having been praised for bluntness, does affect
A saucy roughness, and constrains the garb
Quite from his nature. He cannot flatter, he!

An honest mind and plain—he must speak truth!
And they will take it, so; if not, he's plain.
These kind of knaves I know, which in this plainness
Harbour more craft and more corrupting ends
Than twenty silly-ducking observants
That stretch their duties finely.

KENT
Sir, in good faith, in sincere verity,
Under the allowance of your great aspect
Whose influence like the wreath of radiant fire
On flickering Phoebus' front—

CORNWALL   What mean you by this?

KENT   To go out of my dialect which you discommend
so much. I know, sir, I am no flatterer. He that
beguiled you in a plain accent was a plain knave;
which, for my part, I will not be, though I should
win your displeasure to entreat me to it.

CORNWALL   What was the offence you gave him?

OSWALD   I never gave him any.
It pleased the King his master very late
To strike at me upon his misconstruction,
When he, in pact, and flattering his displeasure,
Tripped me behind. Being down, insulted, railed,
And put upon him such a deal of man
That worthied him, got praises of the King
For him attempting who was self-subdued;
And in fulfilment of this dread exploit
Drew on me here again.

KENT   None of these rogues and cowards
But Ajax is their fool.

CORNWALL   Fetch forth the stocks!
You stubborn ancient knave, you reverend braggart,
We'll teach you—

KENT   Sir, I am too old to learn.
Call not your stocks for me. I serve the King,

On whose employment I was sent to you.
You shall do small respect, show too bold malice
Against the grace and person of my master,
Stocking his messenger.

CORNWALL
Fetch forth the stocks! As I have life and honour,
There shall he sit till noon.

REGAN
Till noon? Till night, my lord, and all night too.

KENT
Why, madam, if I were your father's dog
You should not use me so.

REGAN   Sir, being his knave, I will.

CORNWALL
This is a fellow of the selfsame colour
Our sister speaks of. Come, bring along the stocks.

Stocks brought out

GLOUCESTER
Let me beseech your grace not to do so.
His fault is much, and the good King, his master,
Will check him for it. Your purposed low correction
Is such as basest and contemnedest wretches
For pilferings and most common trespasses
Are punished with. The King must take it ill
That he, so slightly valued in his messenger,
Should have him thus restrained.

CORNWALL   I'll answer that.

REGAN
My sister may receive it thus much worse
To have her gentleman abused, assaulted,

For following her affairs.—Put in his legs.
Come, my lord, away.

Exeunt all but Gloucester and Kent

GLOUCESTER

I am sorry for you, friend. 'Tis the Duke's pleasure,
Whose disposition all the world well knows
Will not be rubbed nor stopped. I'll entreat for you.

KENT

Pray do not, sir. I have watched and travelled hard.
Some time I shall sleep out, the rest I'll whistle.
A good man's fortune may grow out at heels.
Give you good morrow!

GLOUCESTER   The Duke's to blame in this.
It will be ill taken.   *Exit*

KENT

Good King, that must prove the common saying,
You out of Heaven's benediction come
To the warm sun.
Approach, you beacon to this under-globe,
That by your comfortable beams I may
Peruse this letter. Nothing almost sees miracles
But misery. I know it is from Cordelia,
Who has most fortunately been informed
Of my obscurèd course, and (*reading*) 'shall find time
From this ill state of things, seeking to give
Losses their remedies'. All weary and o'erwatched,
Take vantage, heavy eyes, not to behold
This shameful lodging.
Fortune, good night; smile once more; turn your
  wheel.

He sleeps

SCENE III
Open country.

Enter EDGAR

EDGAR

I heard myself proclaimed,
And by the happy hollow of a tree
Escaped the hunt. No port is free, no place
That guard and most unusual vigilance
Do not attend my taking. While I may escape
I will preserve myself; and am bethought
To take the basest and most poor mis-shape
That ever penury, in contempt of man,
Brought near to beast. My face I'll grime with filth,
Blanket my loins, tie all my hairs in knots,
And with presented nakedness outface
The winds and persecutions of the sky.
The country gives me proof and precedent
Of Bedlam beggars who, with roaring voices,
Strike in their numbed and mortified bare arms
Pins, wooden pricks, nails, sprigs of rosemary;
And with this horrible object, from lowly farms,
Poor pelting villages, sheepcotes, and mills
Sometimes with lunatic bans, sometimes with
      prayers,
Enforce their charity: 'Poor Turlygod! Poor Tom!'
That's something yet; Edgar I nothing am.   *Exit*

SCENE IV
Before Gloucester's castle.

KENT *in the stocks*
Enter LEAR, *the* FOOL, *and a* GENTLEMAN

LEAR
  'Tis strange that they should so depart from home
  And not send back my messengers.
GENTLEMAN   As I learned,
  The night before there was no purpose in them
  Of this remove.
KENT   Hail to you, noble master!
LEAR
  Ha!
  Make you this shame your pastime?
KENT   No, my lord.
FOOL   Ha, ha! He wears cruel garters. Horses are
  tied by the heads, dogs and bears by the neck,
  monkeys by the loins, and men by the legs. When
  a man's over-lusty at legs, then he wears wooden
  nether-stocks.
LEAR
  What's he that has so much your place mistaken
  To set you here?
KENT   It is both he and she;
  Your son and daughter.
LEAR   No.
KENT   Yes.
LEAR   No, I say.
KENT   I say yea.
LEAR   No, no, they would not.
KENT   Yes, they have.
LEAR   By Jupiter, I swear no!
KENT
  By Juno, I swear ay!
LEAR   They durst not do it;
  They could not, would not do it; 'tis worse than
    murder
  To do upon respect such violent outrage.
  Resolve me with all modest haste which way

You might deserve or they impose this usage,
Coming from us.

KENT   My lord, when at their home
I did commend your highness' letters to them,
Ere I was risen from the place that showed
My duty kneeling, came there a reeking post,
Stewed in his haste, half breathless, panting forth
From Goneril his mistress salutations;
Delivered letters, spite of intermission,
Which immediately they read. On whose contents
They summoned up their men, straight took horse,
Commanded me to follow and attend
The leisure of their answer, gave me cold looks.
And meeting here the other messenger,
Whose welcome I perceived had poisoned mine—
Being the very fellow who of late
Displayed so saucily against your highness—
Having more man than wit about me, drew.
He raised the house with loud and coward cries.
Your son and daughter found this trespass worth
The shame which here it suffers.

FOOL   Winter's not gone yet if the wild geese fly
that way.

    Fathers that wear rags
        Do make their children blind,
    But fathers that bear bags
        Shall see their children kind.
    Fortune, that arrant whore,
        Never turns the key to the poor.
But for all this you shall have as many dolours
for your daughters as you can tell in a year.

LEAR

O, how this grief swells up toward my heart!
Hysterica passio, down, you climbing sorrow!
Your element's below. Where is this daughter?

KENT   With the Earl, sir, here within.

LEAR   Follow me not; stay here.   *Exit*
GENTLEMAN
  Made you no more offence but what you speak of?
KENT   None.
  How chance the King comes with so small a
    number?
FOOL   If you had been set in the stocks for that
  question, you'd well deserved it.
KENT   Why, Fool?
FOOL   We'll set you to school to an ant to teach you
  there's no labouring in the winter. All that follow
  their noses are led by their eyes, but blind men;
  and there's not a nose among twenty but can smell
  him that's stinking. Let go your hold when a great
  wheel runs down a hill, lest it breaks your neck by
  following. But the great one that goes upward, let
  him draw you after. When a wise man gives you
  better counsel, give me mine again; I would have
  none but knaves use it, since a fool gives it.
    That sir who serves and seeks for gain,
      And follows but for form,
    Will pack when it begins to rain,
      And leave you in the storm;
    But I will tarry, the fool will stay,
      And let the wise man fly.
    The knave turns fool that runs away;
      The fool no knave, perdy. [perchance]
KENT   Where learned you this, Fool?
FOOL   Not in the stocks, fool.

Enter LEAR *and* GLOUCESTER

LEAR
  Deny to speak with me? They are sick; they are
    weary?
  They have travelled all the night? Mere tricks,

The images of revolt and flying-off.
Fetch me a better answer.

GLOUCESTER   My dear lord,
You know the fiery quality of the Duke,
How unremovable and fixed he is
In his own course.

LEAR   Vengeance, plague, death, confusion!
'Fiery'? What 'quality'? Why, Gloucester, Gloucester,
I'd speak with the Duke of Cornwall and his wife.

GLOUCESTER
Well, my good lord, I have informed them so.

LEAR
'Informed them'! Do you understand me, man?

GLOUCESTER   Ay, my good lord.

LEAR
The King would speak with Cornwall, the dear father
Would with his daughter speak, commands—
    tends—service.
Are they 'informed' of this? My breath and blood!
'Fiery'? The 'fiery' Duke? Tell the hot Duke that—
No, but not yet! Maybe he is not well.
Infirmity does ever neglect all office
Whereto our health is bound; we are not ourselves
When nature, being oppressed, commands the mind
To suffer with the body. I'll forbear;
And am fallen out with my more headstrong will
To take the indisposed and sickly fit
For the sound man.—Death on my state! Wherefore
Should he sit here? This act persuades me
That this removal of the Duke and her
Is pretence only. Give me my servant forth.
Go tell the Duke and his wife I'd speak with them—
Now instantly! Bid them come forth and hear me,
Or at their chamber door I'll beat the drum
Till it cries sleep to death.

GLOUCESTER   I would have all well between you. *Exit*

LEAR
  O me, my heart, my rising heart! But down!
FOOL   Cry to it, uncle, as the wench did to the eels
  when she put them in the paste alive. She hit them
  on the coxcombs with a stick and cried 'Down,
  wantons, down!' It was her brother that in pure
  kindness to his horse buttered his hay.

  Enter CORNWALL, REGAN, GLOUCESTER, *and servants*

LEAR
  Good morrow to you both.
CORNWALL   Hail to your grace.

               KENT *is here set at liberty*

REGAN
  I am glad to see your highness.
LEAR
  Regan, I think you are. I know what reason
  I have to think so. If you should not be glad,
  I would divorce me from your mother's tomb,
  Sepulchring an adultress. (*To Kent*) O, are you free?
  Some other time for that.—Belovèd Regan,
  Your sister's naught. O Regan, she has tied
  Sharp-toothed unkindness like a vulture here—

               (*laying his hand on his heart*)

  I can scarce speak to you—you'll not believe
  With how depraved a quality—O Regan!
REGAN
  I pray you, sir, take patience. I have hope
  You less know how to value her desert
  Than she to scant her duty.

LEAR   Say? How is that?

REGAN

I cannot think my sister in the least
Would fail her obligation. If, sir, perchance,
She has restrained the riots of your followers,
'Tis on such ground and to such wholesome end
As clears her from all blame.

LEAR

My curses on her.

REGAN   O sir, you are old.
Nature in you stands on the very verge
Of his confine. You should be ruled and led
By some discretion that discerns your state
Better than you yourself. Therefore I pray you
That to our sister you do make return.
Say you have wronged her.

LEAR   Ask her forgiveness?
Do you but mark how this becomes the house:

(*he kneels*)

'Dear daughter, I confess that I am old;
Age is unnecessary; on my knees I beg
That you will grant me raiment, bed, and food.'

REGAN

Good sir, no more! These are unsightly tricks.
Return you to my sister.

LEAR   (*rising*)   Never, Regan.
She has deprived me now of half my train,
Looked black upon me, struck me with her tongue,
Most serpent-like, upon the very heart.
All the stored vengeances of heaven fall
On her ungrateful top! Strike her young bones,
You taking airs, with lameness!

CORNWALL   Fie, sir, fie!

LEAR

> You nimble lightnings, dart your blinding flames
> Into her scornful eyes! Infect her beauty,
> You fen-sucked fogs drawn by the powerful sun,
> To fall and blister.

REGAN   O the blest gods!

> So will you wish on me when the rash mood is on.

LEAR

> No, Regan, you shall never have my curse.
> Your tender-hefted nature shall not give
> You over to harshness. Her eyes are fierce; but yours
> Do comfort, and not burn. 'Tis not in you
> To grudge my pleasures, to cut off my train,
> To bandy hasty words, to scant my means,
> And, in conclusion, to oppose the bolt
> Against my coming in. You better know
> The offices of nature, bond of childhood,
> Effects of courtesy, dues of gratitude.
> Your half of the kingdom have you not forgot,
> Wherein I you endowed.

REGAN   Good sir, to the purpose.

LEAR

> Who put my man in the stocks?

Tucket within

CORNWALL   What trumpet's that?

REGAN

> I know it—my sister's. This confirms her letter
> That she would soon be here.

Enter OSWALD

                                  Is your lady come?

LEAR

> This is a slave whose easy-borrowed pride

Dwells in the fickle grace of her he follows.

Out, varlet, from my sight!

CORNWALL   What means your grace?

LEAR

Who stocked my servant? Regan, I have good hope
You did not know of it.

Enter GONERIL

                              Who comes here? O heavens!
If you do love old men, if your sweet sway
Allows obedience, if you yourselves are old,
Make it your cause! Send down and take my part!
(To Goneril) You are not ashamed to look upon this
   beard?
O Regan, will you take her by the hand?

GONERIL

Why not by the hand, sir? How have I offended?
All is not offence that indiscretion finds
And dotage terms so.

LEAR   O sides, you are too tough!
Will you yet hold?—How came my man in the stocks?

CORNWALL

I set him there, sir; but his own disorders
Deserved much less advancement.

LEAR   You? Did you?

REGAN

I pray you, father, being weak, seem so.
If till the expiration of your month
You will return and sojourn with my sister,
Dismissing half your train, come then to me.
I am away from home and out of that provision
Which shall be needful for your entertainment.

LEAR

Return to her, and fifty men dismissed!
No, rather I abjure all roofs and choose

To wage against the enmity of the air,
To be a comrade with the wolf and owl—
Necessity's sharp pinch! Return with her?
Why, the hot-blooded France that dowerless took
Our youngest born, I could as well be brought
To knee his throne and, squire-like, pension beg
To keep base life afoot. Return with her!
Persuade me rather to be slave and pack-horse
To this detested groom.

He points to OSWALD

GONERIL   At your choice, sir.
LEAR
I pray you, daughter, do not make me mad.
I will not trouble you, my child. Farewell.
We'll no more meet, no more see one another.
But yet you are my flesh, my blood, my daughter—
Or rather a disease that's in my flesh,
Which I must needs call mine. You are a boil,
A plague-sore, or a swelling full of pus,
In my corrupted blood. But I'll not chide you.
Let shame come when it will, I do not call it.
I do not bid the thunder-bearer shoot,
Nor tell tales of you to high-judging Jove.
Mend when you can, be better at your leisure;
I can be patient, I can stay with Regan,
I and my hundred knights.
REGAN   Not altogether so.
I looked not for you yet, nor am provided
For your fit welcome. Give ear, sir, to my sister;
For those that mingle reason with your passion
Must be content to think you old, and so—
But she knows what she does.
LEAR   Is this well spoken?

REGAN

    I dare affirm it, sir. What, fifty followers?
    Is it not well? What should you need of more?
    Yea, or so many, since both charge and danger
    Speak against so great a number? How in one house
    Should many people under two commands
    Hold amity? 'Tis hard, almost impossible.

GONERIL

    Why might not you, my lord, receive attendance
    From those that she calls servants, or from mine?

REGAN

    Why not, my lord? If then they chanced to slack you,
    We could control them. If you will come to me,
    For now I spy a danger, I entreat you
    To bring but five-and-twenty; to no more
    Will I give place or notice.

LEAR

    I gave you all—

REGAN   And in good time you gave it.

LEAR

    Made you my guardians, my depositaries;
    But kept a reservation to be followed
    With such a number. What, must I come to you
    With five-and-twenty—Regan, said you so?

REGAN

    And speak it again, my lord. No more with me.

LEAR

    Those wicked creatures yet do look well-favoured
    When others are more wicked. Not being the worst
    Stands in some rank of praise. (*To Goneril*) I'll go
      with you.
    Your fifty yet does double five-and-twenty,
    And you are twice her love.

GONERIL   Hear me, my lord;
    What need you five-and-twenty, ten, or five
    To follow, in a house where twice so many
    Have a command to tend you?

REGAN   What need one?

LEAR

O, reason not the need! Our basest beggars
Are in the poorest thing superfluous.
Allow not nature more than nature needs—
Man's life is cheap as beast's. You are a lady;
If only to go warm were gorgeous,
Why, nature needs not what you gorgeous wear,
Which scarcely keeps you warm. But for true need—
You heavens, give me that patience, patience I need!
You see me here, you gods, a poor old man,
As full of grief as age, wretched in both;
If it is you that stirs these daughters' hearts
Against their father, fool me not so much
To bear it tamely; touch me with noble anger,
And let not women's weapons, water drops,
Stain my man's cheeks. No, you unnatural hags,
I will have such revenges on you both
That all the world shall—I will do such things—
What they are yet I know not; but they shall be
The terrors of the earth. You think I'll weep.
No, I'll not weep.
I have full cause of weeping;

(storm and tempest)

but this heart
Shall break into a hundred thousand pieces
Or ere I'll weep. O Fool, I shall go mad!
Exeunt Lear, Gloucester, Kent, the Fool, and Gentleman

CORNWALL   Let us withdraw; it will be a storm.

REGAN

This house is little; the old man and his people
Cannot be well bestowed.

GONERIL

'Tis his own blame; has put himself from rest
And must needs taste his folly.

REGAN
    As an individual, I'll receive him gladly,
    But not one follower.
GONERIL   So am I purposed.
    Where is my lord of Gloucester?
CORNWALL
    Followed the old man forth. He has returned.

                    Enter GLOUCESTER

GLOUCESTER
    The King is in high rage.
CORNWALL   Whither is he going?
GLOUCESTER
    He calls to horse; but will I know not whither.
CORNWALL
    'Tis best to give him way. He leads himself.
GONERIL
    My lord, entreat him by no means to stay.
GLOUCESTER
    Alas, the night comes on and the bleak winds
    Do sorely ruffle. For many miles about
    There's scarce a bush.
REGAN   O sir, to wilful men
    The injuries that they themselves procure
    Must be their schoolmasters. Shut up your doors.
    He is attended with a desperate train,
    And what they may incense him to, being apt
    To have his ear abused, wisdom bids fear.
CORNWALL
    Shut up your doors, my lord; 'tis a wild night.
    My Regan counsels well. Come out of the storm.
                                                    Exeunt

Act III

SCENE I
A heath.

Storm still. Enter KENT *and a* GENTLEMAN
by opposite doors

KENT   Who's there besides foul weather?

GENTLEMAN
One minded like the weather, most unquietly.

KENT   I know you. Where's the King?

GENTLEMAN
Contending with the fretful elements:
Bids the wind blow the earth into the sea,
Or swell the curlèd waters above the main,
That things might change or cease; tears his white
  hair,
Which the impetuous blasts with eyeless rage
Catch in their fury and make nothing of;
Strives in his little world of man to out-storm
The to-and-fro conflicting wind and rain.
This night, wherein the cub-drawn bear would couch,
The lion and the belly-pinchèd wolf
Keep their fur dry, unbonneted he runs
And bids what will take all.

KENT   But who is with him?

GENTLEMAN
None but the Fool, who labours to out-jest
His heart-struck injuries.

KENT   Sir, I do know you,
  And dare upon the warrant of my note
  Command a dear thing to you. There is division—
  Although as yet the face of it is covered
  With mutual cunning—between Albany and
      Cornwall;
  Who have—as who have not that their great stars
  Throned and set high—servants, who seem no less,
  Who are to France the spies and speculations
  Intelligent of our state. What has been seen,
  Either in huffs and plottings of the Dukes,
  Or the hard rein which both of them have borne
  Against the old kind King, or something deeper,
  Whereof, perchance, these are but furnishings—
  But true it is, from France there comes a power
  Into this scattered kingdom. These already,
  Wise in our negligence, have secret feet
  In some of our best ports and are at point
  To show their open banner. Now to you:
  If on my credit you dare build so far
  To make your speed to Dover, you shall find
  Some that will thank you making just report
  Of how unnatural and bemadding sorrow
  The King has cause to complain.
  I am a gentleman of blood and breeding,
  And from some knowledge and assurance offer
  This office to you.
GENTLEMAN
  I will talk further with you.
KENT   No, do not.
  For confirmation that I am much more
  Than my out-wall, open this purse and take
  What it contains. If you shall see Cordelia—
  As fear not but you shall—show her this ring,
  And she will tell you who that fellow is

That yet you do not know. Fie on this storm!
I will go seek the King.
GENTLEMAN
Give me your hand. Have you no more to say?
KENT
Few words, but to effect more than all yet:
That when we have found the King—in which your
    pain
That way, I'll this—he that first lights on him
Holla the other.   *Exeunt by opposite doors*

SCENE II
The same.

Storm still. Enter LEAR *and the* FOOL

LEAR
Blow, winds, and crack your cheeks! Rage! Blow!
You cataracts and hurricanoes, spout
Till you have drenched our steeples, drowned the
    cocks!
You sulphurous and thought-executing fires,
Precursors of oak-cleaving thunderbolts,
Singe my white head! And you all-shaking thunder,
Strike flat the thick rotundity of the world,
Crack Nature's moulds, all seed-beds spill at once
That makes ungrateful man!
FOOL   O uncle, court holy-water in a dry house is
better than this rain-water out of door. Good uncle,
in; ask your daughters' blessing. Here's a night
pities neither wise men nor fools.
LEAR
Rumble your bellyful! Spit, fire! Spout, rain!
Nor rain, wind, thunder, fire are my daughters.

I tax not you, you elements, with unkindness;
I never gave you kingdom, called you children.
You owe me no subscription; then let fall
Your horrible pleasure. Here I stand, your slave,
A poor, infirm, weak, and despised old man.
But yet I call you servile ministers,
That will with two pernicious daughters join
Your high-engendered battles against a head
So old and white as this. O, ho! 'Tis foul!

FOOL   He that has a house to put his head in has a
good headpiece:
　　The cod-piece that will house
　　　Before the head has any,
　　The head and he shall louse;
　　　So beggars marry many.
　　The man that makes his toe
　　　What he his heart should make,
　　Shall of a corn cry woe,
　　　And turn his sleep to wake.
For there was never yet fair woman but she made
mouths in a glass.

Enter KENT

LEAR

No, I will be the pattern of all patience.
I will say nothing.

KENT   Who's there?

FOOL   Surely, here's grace and a cod-piece—that's a
wise man and a fool.

KENT

Alas, sir, are you here? Things that love night
Love not such nights as these. The wrathful skies
Frighten the very wanderers of the dark
And make them keep their caves. Since I was man,

Such sheets of fire, such bursts of horrid thunder,
Such groans of roaring wind and rain I never
Remember to have heard. Man's nature cannot carry
The affliction nor the fear.

LEAR   Let the great gods
That keep this dreadful pother over our heads
Find out their enemies now. Tremble, you wretch
That have within you undivulgèd crimes
Unwhipped of justice. Hide, you bloody hand,
You perjured, and you simular of virtue
That are incestuous. Wretch, to pieces shake,
That under covert and convenient seeming
Has practised on man's life. Close pent-up guilts,
Rive your concealing continents, and cry
These dreadful summoners grace. I am a man
More sinned against than sinning.

KENT   Alas, bare-headed?
Gracious my lord, hard by here is a hovel;
Some friendship will it lend against the tempest.
Repose you there while I to this hard house—
Harder than the stones whereof it is raised;
Which even but now, demanding after you,
Denied me to come in—return and force
Their scanted courtesy.

LEAR   My wits begin to turn.
Come on, my boy. How do you, boy? You cold?
I am cold myself. Where is this straw, my fellow?
The art of our necessities is strange
And can make vile things precious. Come, your
    hovel.
Poor fool and knave, I have one part in my heart
That's sorry yet for you.

FOOL   (*sings*)
    He that has but a little tiny wit,
    With heigh-ho, the wind and the rain,

Must make content with his fortunes fit,
Though the rain it should rain every day.
LEAR   True, boy. Come, bring us to this hovel.

Exeunt Lear and Kent

FOOL   This is a brave night to cool a courtesan. I'll
speak a prophecy ere I go:
When priests are more in word than matter,
When brewers mar their malt with water,
When nobles are their tailors' tutors,
No heretics burned but wenches' suitors—
Then shall the realm of Albiòn
Come to great confusiòn.

When every case in law is right,
No squire in debt and no poor knight,
When slanders do not live in tongues,
And cutpurses come not to throngs,
When usurers tell their gold in the field,
And bawds and whores do churches build—
Then comes the time, who lives to see't,
That going shall be used with feet.
This prophecy Merlin shall make; for I live before
his time.   *Exit*

SCENE III
Gloucester's castle.

Enter GLOUCESTER *and* EDMUND *with lights*

GLOUCESTER   Alas, alas, Edmund, I like not this
unnatural dealing. When I desired their leave that I
might pity him, they took from me the use of my
own house, charged me on pain of perpetual
displeasure neither to speak of him, entreat for
him, or any way sustain him.

EDMUND   Most savage and unnatural!

GLOUCESTER   Go to. Say you nothing. There is division
between the Dukes; and a worse matter than that. I
have received a letter this night; it is dangerous to
be spoken; I have locked the letter in my closet.
These injuries the King now bears will be revenged
home. There is part of a force already on foot. We
must incline to the King. I will look to him and
privily relieve him. Go you and maintain talk with
the Duke, that my charity is not of him perceived.
If he asks for me, I am ill and gone to bed. If I die
for it, as no less is threatened me, the King my old
master must be relieved. There are strange things
toward, Edmund. Pray you, be careful.   *Exit*

EDMUND

This courtesy forbidden shall the Duke
Instantly know, and of that letter too.
This seems a fair deserving, and must draw me
That which my father loses—no less than all.
The younger rises when the old does fall.   *Exit*

SCENE IV
The heath, before a hovel.

Enter LEAR, KENT, *and the* FOOL

KENT

Here is the place, my lord; good my lord, enter.
The tyranny of the open night is too rough
For nature to endure.

Storm still

LEAR   Let me alone.

KENT

Good my lord, enter here.

LEAR   Will you break my heart?

KENT

I had rather break my own. Good my lord, enter.

LEAR

You think it much that this contentious storm
Invades us to the skin; so it is to you.
But where the greater malady is fixed
The lesser is scarce felt. You would shun a bear;
But if your flight lay toward the roaring sea
You'd meet the bear in the mouth. When the mind's
    free
The body's delicate; this tempest in my mind
Does from my senses take all feeling else
Save what beats there.—Filial ingratitude!
Is it not as this mouth should tear this hand
For lifting food to it? But I will punish home.
No, I will weep no more! In such a night
To shut me out! Pour on; I will endure.
In such a night as this! O Regan, Goneril!
Your old kind father, whose frank heart gave all!
O, that way madness lies; let me shun that;
No more of that!

KENT   Good my lord, enter here.

LEAR

Pray go in yourself; seek your own ease.
This tempest will not give me leave to ponder
On things would hurt me more; but I'll go in.
(*To the Fool*) In, boy, go first.—You houseless
    poverty—
Nay, get you in. I'll pray and then I'll sleep.

                       Exit the Fool.

Poor naked wretches, wheresoever you are,
That bide the pelting of this pitiless storm,

How shall your houseless heads and unfed sides,
Your loop-holed windowed raggedness, defend you
From seasons such as these? O, I have taken
Too little care of this! Take physic, pomp;
Expose yourself to feel what wretches feel,
That you may shake the superflux to them
And show the heavens more just.

EDGAR   (*within*)
Fathom and half, fathom and half! Poor Tom!

Enter the FOOL *from the hovel*

FOOL   Come not in here, uncle; here's a spirit. Help me,
help me!
KENT   Give me your hand. Who's there?
FOOL   A spirit, a spirit! He says his name's Poor Tom.
KENT   What are you that do grumble there in the straw?
Come forth.

Enter EDGAR *disguised as Poor Tom*

EDGAR   Away! The foul fiend follows me.
Through the sharp hawthorn blow the cold winds.
Hum! Go to your bed and warm you.
LEAR   Did you give all to your daughters? And are you
come to this?
EDGAR   Who gives anything to Poor Tom? whom the
foul fiend has led through fire and through flame,
through ford and whirlpool, over bog and quagmire,
that has laid knives under his pillow and halters in
his pew, set ratsbane by his porridge, made him
proud of heart, to ride on a bay trotting horse over
four-inched bridges to course his own shadow for a
traitor. Bless your five wits! Tom's a-cold. O do, de,
do, de, do, de. Bless you from whirlwinds, star-

blasting, and infection! Do Poor Tom some charity,
whom the foul fiend vexes. There could I have him
now, and there, and there again, and there.

Storm still

LEAR

What have his daughters brought him to this pass?
Could you save nothing? Would you give them all?

FOOL   Nay, he reserved a blanket; else we had been all
shamed.

LEAR

Now all the plagues that in the pendulous air
Hang fated o'er men's faults light on your daughters!

KENT   He has no daughters, sir.

LEAR

Death, traitor! Nothing could have subdued nature
To such a lowness but his unkind daughters.
Is it the fashion that discarded fathers
Should have thus little mercy on their flesh?
Judicious punishment! It was this flesh begot
Those pelican daughters.

EDGAR

Pillicock sat on Pillicock Hill.
Alow, alow, loo, loo!

FOOL   This cold night will turn us all to fools and
madmen.

EDGAR   Take heed of the foul fiend, obey your parents,
keep your word's justice, swear not, commit not with
man's sworn spouse, set not your sweetheart on
proud array. Tom's a-cold.

LEAR   What have you been?

EDGAR   A servingman, proud in heart and mind, that
curled my hair, wore gloves in my cap, served the
lust of my mistress' heart and did the act of darkness

with her; swore as many oaths as I spoke words and
broke them in the sweet face of heaven. One that
slept in the contriving of lust and waked to do it.
Wine loved I deeply, dice dearly, and in woman out-
paramoured the Turk. False of heart, light of ear,
bloody of hand; hog in sloth, fox in stealth, wolf in
greediness, dog in madness, lion in prey. Let not the
creaking of shoes nor the rustling of silks betray your
poor heart to woman. Keep your foot out of brothels,
your hand out of petticoats, your pen from lenders'
books, and defy the foul fiend.
   Still through the hawthorn blows the cold wind,
   Says suum, mun, nonny.
Dolphin, my boy, boy, sessa! Let him trot by.

Storm still

LEAR   You were better in a grave than to answer with
   your uncovered body this extremity of the skies. Is
   man no more than this? Consider him well. You owe
   the worm no silk, the beast no hide, the sheep no
   wool, the cat no perfume. Ha! Here's three of us are
   sophisticated. You are the thing itself! Unaccommo-
   dated man is no more than such a poor, bare, forked
   animal as you are. Off, off, you lendings! Come
   unbutton here.

He tears off his clothes

FOOL   Pray, uncle, be contented; 'tis a nasty night to
   swim in. Now a little fire in a wild field were like an
   old lecher's heart—a small spark, all the rest of his
   body cold. Look, here comes a walking fire.

Enter GLOUCESTER *with a torch*

EDGAR   This is the foul fiend Flibbertigibbet. He begins
at curfew and walks till the first cock. He gives us
cataracts, squints the eye and makes the harelip,
mildews the white wheat, and hurts the poor creature
of earth.
> St. Withold footed thrice the wold;
> He met the nightmare and her nine-fold,
> Bid her alight and her troth plight—
> And begone, witch, take you off!

KENT   How fares your grace?

LEAR   What's he?

KENT   *(to Gloucester)* Who's there? What is it you
seek?

GLOUCESTER   What are you there? Your names?

EDGAR   Poor Tom, that eats the swimming frog, the
toad, the tadpole, the lizard and the water newt—
that in the fury of his heart, when the foul fiend
rages, eats cowdung for salad, swallows the old rat
and the ditch-dog, drinks the green mantle of the
standing pool; who is whipped from tithing to tithing
and stock-punished and imprisoned; who has had
three suits to his back, six shirts to his body,
> Horse to ride and weapon to wear—
> But mice and rats and such small deer
> Have been Tom's food for seven long year.
Beware my follower! Peace, Smulkin! Peace, you fiend!

GLOUCESTER   What, has your grace no better company?

EDGAR   The prince of darkness is a gentleman; Modo
he's called, and Mahu.

GLOUCESTER
> Our flesh and blood, my lord, is grown so vile
> That it does hate what begets it.

EDGAR   Poor Tom's a-cold.

GLOUCESTER
  Go in with me. My duty cannot suffer
  To obey in all your daughters' hard commands;
  Though their injunction is to bar my doors
  And let this tyrannous night take hold upon you,
  Yet have I ventured to come seek you out
  And bring you where both fire and food are ready.

LEAR
  First let me talk with this philosopher.
  (To Edgar) What is the cause of thunder?

KENT   Good my lord,
  Take his offer, go into the house.

LEAR
  I'll talk a word with this same learnèd Theban.
  (To Edgar) What is your study?

EDGAR   How to prevent the fiend and to kill vermin.

LEAR   Let me ask you one word in private.

KENT
  Importune him once more to go, my lord.
  His wits begin to unsettle.

GLOUCESTER   Can you blame him?—

Storm still

  His daughters seek his death. Ah, that good Kent,
  He said it would be thus, poor banished man!
  You say the King grows mad; I'll tell you, friend,
  I am almost mad myself. I had a son,
  Now outlawed from my blood; he sought my life
  But lately, very late. I loved him, friend,
  No father his son dearer. True to tell you,
  The grief has crazed my wits. What a night's this!—
  I do beseech your grace—

LEAR   O, cry you mercy, sir.
  (*To Edgar*) Noble philosopher, your company.
EDGAR   Tom's a-cold.
GLOUCESTER   In, fellow, there, into the hovel; keep
  warm.
LEAR
  Come, let's in all.
KENT   This way, my lord.
LEAR   With him!
  I will keep still with my philosopher.
KENT   Good my lord, soothe him: let him take the
  fellow.
GLOUCESTER   Take him you on.
KENT   Fellow, come on. Go along with us.
LEAR   Come, good Athenian.
GLOUCESTER   No words, no words! Hush!
EDGAR
    Child Roland to the dark tower came;
    His word was ever, 'Fie, foh, and fum,
    I smell the blood of a British man.'   *Exeunt*

SCENE V
Gloucester's castle.

Enter CORNWALL *and* EDMUND

CORNWALL   I will have my revenge ere I depart his
  house.
EDMUND   How, my lord, I may be censured that nature
  thus gives way to loyalty, something fears me to
  think of.
CORNWALL   I now perceive it was not altogether your
  brother's evil disposition made him seek his death;
  but a provoking merit set a-work by a reprovable
  badness in himself.

EDMUND   How malicious is my fortune that I must
    repent to be just! This is the letter he spoke of, which
    proves him an intelligent party to the advantages of
    France. O heavens! that this treason were not, or not I
    the detector.
CORNWALL   Go with me to the Duchess.
EDMUND   If the matter of this paper is certain, you have
    mighty business in hand.
CORNWALL   True or false, it has made you Earl of
    Gloucester. Seek out where your father is, that he
    may be ready for our apprehension.
EDMUND (*aside*) If I find him comforting the King it will
    stuff his suspicion more fully. (*Aloud*) I will
    persevere in my course of loyalty, though the conflict
    is sore between that and my blood.
CORNWALL   I will lay trust upon you, and you shall find
    a dearer father in my love.   *Exeunt*

SCENE VI
An outbuilding of the castle.

Enter KENT *and* GLOUCESTER

GLOUCESTER   Here is better than the open air. Take it
    thankfully; I will piece out the comfort with what
    addition I can. I will not be long from you.
KENT   All the power of his wits have given way to his
    impatience. The gods reward your kindness!
                                          Exit Gloucester

Enter LEAR, EDGAR, *and the* FOOL

EDGAR   Fraterretto calls me and tells me Nero is an
    angler in the lake of darkness. Pray, innocent, and
    beware the foul fiend.

FOOL   Pray, uncle, tell me whether a madman is a
gentleman or a yeoman.

LEAR   A king, a king!

FOOL   No! He's a yeoman that has a gentleman to his
son; for he's a mad yeoman that sees his son a
gentleman before him.

LEAR

To have a thousand with red burning spits
Come hissing in upon them!

EDGAR   The foul fiend bites my back.

FOOL   He's mad that trusts in the tameness of a wolf,
a horse's health, a boy's love, or a whore's oath.

LEAR

It shall be done; I will arraign them straight.
(To Edgar)
Come, sit you here, most learnèd justicer.
(To the Fool)
You sapient sir, sit here. No, you she-foxes—

EDGAR   Look where he stands and glares! Want you
eyes at trial, madam?
        (sings)
                Come o'er the burn, Bessy, to me.

FOOL   *(sings)*   Her boat has a leak
                And she must not speak
                Why she dares not come over to thee.

EDGAR   The foul fiend haunts Poor Tom in the voice of
a nightingale. Hop dance cries in Tom's belly for two
white herring. Croak not, black angel! I have no food for
you.

KENT

How do you, sir? Stand you not so amazed.
Will you lie down and rest upon the cushions?

LEAR

I'll see their trial first; bring in their evidence.
(To Edgar)

You robed man of justice, take your place.
(*To the Fool*)
And you, his yokefellow of equity,
Bench by his side. (*To Kent*) You are of the
  commission;
Sit you too.

EDGAR   Let us deal justly.
    Sleep or wake you, jolly shepherd?
      Your sheep are in the corn.
    And for one blast of your little mouth
      Your sheep shall take no harm.
  Pur, the cat is grey.

LEAR   Arraign her first. 'Tis Goneril! I here take my oath
before this honourable assembly she kicked the poor
King her father.

FOOL   Come hither, mistress. Is your name Goneril?

LEAR   She cannot deny it.

FOOL   Cry you mercy, I took you for a joint-stool.

LEAR
  And here's another whose warped looks proclaim
  What store her heart is made of. Stop her there!
  Arms, arms, sword, fire! Corruption in the place!
  False justicer, why have you let her escape?

EDGAR   Bless your five wits!

KENT
  O pity! Sir, where is the patience now
  That you so oft have boasted to retain?

EDGAR   (*aside*)
  My tears begin to take his part so much
  They mar my counterfeiting.

LEAR
  The little dogs and all—
  Tray, Blanch, and Sweetheart—see, they bark at me.

EDGAR   Tom will throw his head at them. Be gone, you
curs!

Be your mouth or black or white,
Tooth that poisons if it bite,
Mastiff, greyhound, mongrel grim,
Hound or spaniel, brach or lym, [bitch or
   blood-hound]
Or bobtail tike, or trundle-tail,
Tom will make him weep and wail;
For, with throwing thus my head,
Dogs leapt the hatch and all are fled.
Do, de, de, de. Sesa! Come, march to wakes and fairs
and market-towns. Poor Tom, your horn is dry.

LEAR   Then let them anatomize Regan, see what breeds
about her heart. Is there any cause in nature that
makes these hard hearts? You, sir, I entertain for one
of my hundred. Only I do not like the fashion of your
garments. You will say they are Persian; but let them
be changed.

KENT

Now, good my lord, lie here and rest awhile.

LEAR   Make no noise, make no noise; draw the curtains.
So, so. We'll go to supper in the morning.

FOOL   And I'll go to bed at noon.

Enter GLOUCESTER

GLOUCESTER

Come hither, friend. Where is the King my master?

KENT

Here, sir; but trouble him not; his wits are gone.

GLOUCESTER

Good friend, I pray you take him in your arms;
I have o'erheard a plot of death upon him.

There is a litter ready; lay him in it
And drive toward Dover, friend, where you shall meet
Both welcome and protection. Take up your master;
If you should dally half an hour, his life,
With yours and all that offer to defend him,
Stand in assurèd loss. Take up, take up,
And follow me, that will to some provision
Give you quick conduct.

KENT   Oppressèd nature sleeps.
This rest might yet have balmed your broken sinews
Which, if convenience will not allow,
Stand in hard cure. *(To the Fool)* Come, help to bear
    your master.
You must not stay behind.

GLOUCESTER   Come, come, away!
              Exeunt Kent, Gloucester, and the Fool,
                     bearing off Lear

EDGAR
When we our betters see bearing our woes,
We scarcely think our miseries our foes.
Who alone suffers, suffers most in the mind,
Leaving free things and happy shows behind;
But then the mind much sufferance does o'erskip
When grief has mates, and bearing fellowship.
How light and portable my pain seems now,
When that which makes me bend makes the King
    bow—
He childed as I fathered. Tom, away!
Mark the high noises, and yourself betray
When false opinion, whose wrong thought defiles you,
In your just proof repeals and reconciles you.
What will hap more tonight, safe escape the King!
Lurk, lurk!   *Exit*

SCENE VII
Gloucester's castle.

Enter CORNWALL, REGAN, GONERIL, EDMUND, *and
servants*

CORNWALL *(to Goneril)* Post speedily to my lord your
husband, show him this letter. The army of France has
landed.—Seek out the traitor Gloucester.

Exeunt servants

REGAN   Hang him instantly!

GONERIL   Pluck out his eyes!

CORNWALL   Leave him to my displeasure. Edmund,
keep you our sister company; the revenges we are
bound to take upon your traitorous father are not fit
for your beholding. Advise the Duke where you are
going to a most speedy preparation; we are bound to
the like. Our posts shall be swift and intelligent between us. Farewell, dear sister. Farewell, my lord of
Gloucester.

Enter OSWALD

How now? Where's the King?

OSWALD

My lord of Gloucester has conveyed him hence,
Some five- or six-and-thirty of his knights,
Hot seekers after him, met him at gate,
Who with some others of the lord's dependants
Are gone with him towards Dover, where they boast
To have well-armèd friends.

CORNWALL   Get horses for your mistress.   *Exit Oswald*

GONERIL   Farewell, sweet lord, and sister.

CORNWALL

Edmund, farewell.

Exeunt Goneril and Edmund
Go seek the traitor Gloucester.
Pinion him like a thief; bring him before us.
Exeunt servants
Though well we may not pass upon his life
Without the form of justice, yet our power
Shall do a courtesy to our wrath, which men
May blame but not control.

Enter GLOUCESTER, *brought in by servants*

Who's there? The traitor?
REGAN   Ungrateful fox, 'tis he!
CORNWALL   Bind fast his corky arms.
GLOUCESTER
What mean your graces? Good my friends, consider
You are my guests. Do me no foul play, friends.
CORNWALL
Bind him, I say.
REGAN   Hard, hard! O filthy traitor!
GLOUCESTER
Unmerciful lady as you are, I'm none.
CORNWALL
To this chair bind him. Villain, you shall find—

REGAN *plucks his beard*

GLOUCESTER
By the kind gods, 'tis most ignobly done
To pluck me by the beard.
REGAN
So white, and such a traitor!
GLOUCESTER   Wicked lady,
These hairs which you do ravish from my chin
Will quicken and accuse you. I am your host;
With robbers' hands my hospitable favours
You should not ruffle thus. What will you do?

CORNWALL

Come, sir; what letters had you late from France?

REGAN

Be simple-answered, for we know the truth.

CORNWALL

And what confederacy have you with the traitors
Late footed in the kingdom—

REGAN

To whose hands you have sent the lunatic King.
Speak!

GLOUCESTER

I have a letter guessingly set down
Which came from one that's of a neutral heart
And not from one opposed.

CORNWALL   Cunning.

REGAN   And false.

CORNWALL

Where have you sent the King?

GLOUCESTER   To Dover.

REGAN

Wherefore to Dover? Were you not charged at peril—

CORNWALL

Wherefore to Dover? Let him answer that.

GLOUCESTER

I am tied to the stake, and I must stand the course.

REGAN   Wherefore to Dover?

GLOUCESTER

Because I would not see your cruel nails
Pluck out his poor old eyes; nor your fierce sister
In his anointed flesh stick boarish fangs.
The sea, with such a storm as his bare head
In hell-black night endured, would have buoyed up
And quenched the starry fires;
Yet, poor old heart, he helped the heavens to rain.

If wolves had at your gate howled that dread time
You should have said, 'Good porter, turn the key;
All cruels else do yield'. But I shall see
The wingèd Vengeance overtake such children.

CORNWALL
See it shall you never. Fellows, hold the chair.
Upon these eyes of yours I'll set my foot.

GLOUCESTER
He that will think to live till he is old
Give me some help!—O, cruel! O, you gods!

REGAN
One side will mock another. The other too!

CORNWALL
If you see Vengeance—

FIRST SERVANT   Hold your hand, my lord!
I have served you ever since I was a child;
But better service have I never done you
Than now to bid you hold.

REGAN   How now, you dog!

FIRST SERVANT
If you did wear a beard upon your chin
I'd shake it on this quarrel.

(CORNWALL *draws his sword*)

                              What do you mean?

CORNWALL My villain!

He thrusts at him

FIRST SERVANT (*drawing his sword*)
Nay then, come on, and take the chance of anger.

He wounds CORNWALL

REGAN

Give me your sword. A peasant stand up thus!

She takes a sword and stabs him from behind

FIRST SERVANT

O, I am slain! My lord, you have one eye left
To see some mischief on him. O!   *He dies*

CORNWALL

Lest it see more, prevent it. Out, vile jelly!
Where is your lustre now?

GLOUCESTER

All dark and comfortless. Where's my son Edmund?
Edmund, enkindle all the sparks of nature
To quit this horrid act.

REGAN   Out, treacherous villain!
You call on him that hates you. It was he
That made the opening of your treasons to us;
Who is too good to pity you.

GLOUCESTER

O my follies! Then Edgar was abused.
Kind gods, forgive me that and prosper him.

REGAN

Go thrust him out at gates and let him smell
His way to Dover.   *Exit a servant with Gloucester*
                              How is it, my lord? How look you?

CORNWALL

I have received a hurt. Follow me, lady.
Turn out that eyeless villain. Throw this slave
Upon the dunghill. Regan, I bleed apace.
Untimely comes this hurt. Give me your arm.
                        Exit Cornwall, supported by Regan

SECOND SERVANT

I'll never care what wickedness I do
If this man comes to good.

THIRD SERVANT   If she lives long,
  And in the end meets the old course of death,
  Women will all turn monsters.
SECOND SERVANT
  Let's follow the old Earl, and get the Bedlam
  To lead him where he would; his roguish madness
  Allows itself to anything.
THIRD SERVANT
  Go you. I'll fetch some flax and whites of eggs
  To apply to his bleeding face. Now heaven help him!
                                 Exeunt

Act IV

SCENE 1
The heath.

Enter EDGAR

EDGAR

    Yet better thus, and known to be contemned,
    Than still contemned and flattered. To be worst,
    The lowest and most dejected thing of fortune,
    Stands still in esperance, lives not in fear.
    The lamentable change is from the best;
    The worst returns to laughter. Welcome, then,
    You unsubstantial air that I embrace!
    The wretch that you have blown unto the worst
    Owes nothing to your blasts.

Enter GLOUCESTER, *led by an* OLD MAN

                               But who comes here?
    My father, poorly led! World, world, O world!
    But that your strange mutations make us hate you
    Life would not yield to age.

OLD MAN   O my good lord,
    I have been your tenant and your father's tenant
    These fourscore years!

GLOUCESTER

    Away! Get you away! Good friend, be gone.
    Your comforts can do me no good at all;
    You they may hurt.

OLD MAN   You cannot see your way.

GLOUCESTER
I have no way and therefore want no eyes;
I stumbled when I saw. Full oft 'tis seen
Our means secure us, and our mere defects
Prove our commodities. O dear son Edgar,
The food of your abusèd father's wrath!
Might I but live to see you in my touch
I'd say I had eyes again.

OLD MAN   How now? Who's there?

EDGAR (aside)
O gods? Who is it can say 'I am at the worst'?
I am worse than ever I was.

OLD MAN   'Tis poor mad Tom.

EDGAR (aside)
And worse I may be yet. The worst is not,
So long as we can say 'This is the worst'.

OLD MAN
Fellow, where go you?

GLOUCESTER   Is it a beggar-man?

OLD MAN   Madman and beggar too.

GLOUCESTER
He has some reason, else he could not beg.
In the last night's storm I such a fellow saw
Who made me think a man a worm. My son
Came then into my mind; and yet my mind
Was then scarce friends with him. I have heard
    more since.
As flies to wanton boys are we to the gods;
They kill us for their sport.

EDGAR (aside)   How should this be?
Bad is the trade that must play fool to sorrow,
Angering itself and others. (Aloud) Bless you,
    master!

GLOUCESTER
Is that the naked fellow?

OLD MAN   Ay, my lord.

GLOUCESTER

Then pray get you away. If for my sake
You will overtake us hence a mile or twain
In the way toward Dover, do it for ancient love,
And bring some covering for this naked soul,
Which I'll entreat to lead me.

OLD MAN   Alas, sir, he is mad.

GLOUCESTER

'Tis the time's plague when madmen lead the blind.
Do as I bid you, or rather do your pleasure.
Above the rest, begone.

OLD MAN

I'll bring him the best apparel that I have,
Come of it what will.   *Exit*

GLOUCESTER   Sir naked fellow!

EDGAR

Poor Tom's a-cold. (*Aside*) I cannot daub it further.

GLOUCESTER   Come hither, fellow.

EDGAR   (*aside*)

And yet I must. (*Aloud*) Bless your sweet eyes, they
bleed.

GLOUCESTER   Know you the way to Dover?

EDGAR   Both stile and gate, horse-way and footpath,
Poor Tom has been scared out of his good wits. Bless
you, good man's son, from the foul fiend. Five fiends
have been in Poor Tom at once: of lust, as Obidicut;
Hobbididence, prince of dumbness; Mahu, of
stealing; Modo, of murder; Flibbertigibbet, of
mopping and mowing, who since possesses
chambermaids and waiting-women. So bless you,
master!

GLOUCESTER

Here, take this purse, you whom the heavens'
plagues

Have humbled to all strokes. That I am wretched
 Makes you the happier. Heavens deal so still!
Let the superfluous and lust-dieted man
That slaves your ordinance, that will not see
Because he does not feel, feel your power quickly!
So distribution should undo excess
And each man have enough. Do you know Dover?

EDGAR   Ay, master.

GLOUCESTER

There is a cliff whose high and bending head
Looks fearfully in the confinèd deep;
Bring me but to the very brim of it
And I'll repair the misery you do bear
With something rich about me. From that place
I shall no leading need.

EDGAR   Give me your arm;
Poor Tom shall lead you.   *Exeunt*

SCENE II
Before Albany's palace.

Enter GONERIL *and* EDMUND

GONERIL

Welcome, my lord. I marvel our mild husband
Not met us on the way.

Enter OSWALD

                        Now, where's your master?

OSWALD

Madam, within; but never man so changed.
I told him of the army that has landed.
He smiled at it. I told him you were coming.

His answer was 'The worse'. Of Gloucester's
   treachery
And of the loyal service of his son
When I informed him, then he called me sot
And told me I had turned the wrong side out.
What most he should dislike seems pleasant to him;
What like, offensive.
GONERIL   *(to Edmund)* Then shall you go no further.
It is the cowish terror of his spirit
That dares not undertake. He'll not feel wrongs
Which tie him to an answer. Our wishes on the way
May prove effects. Back, Edmund, to my brother!
Hasten his musters and conduct his forces.
I must change names at home and give the distaff
Into my husband's hands. This trusty servant
Shall pass between us; ere long you'll likely hear,
If you dare venture in your own behalf,
A mistress's command. Wear this;
    (gives a favour)   spare speech.
Incline your head; this kiss, if it dares speak,
Would stretch your spirits up into the air.
Imagine; and fare you well.
EDMUND

Yours in the ranks of death.
GONERIL   My most dear Gloucester!
                              Exit Edmund

O, the difference of man and man!
To you a woman's services are due;
A fool usurps my bed.
OSWALD   Madam, here comes my lord.
                                   Exit

Enter ALBANY

GONERIL
  I have been worth the whistling.
ALBANY   O Goneril,
  You are not worth the dust which the rude wind
  Blows in your face. I fear your disposition:
  That nature which contemns its origin
  Cannot be bordered certain in itself.
  She that herself will sliver and disbranch
  From her material sap perforce must wither
  And come to deadly use.
GONERIL   No more; the text is foolish.
ALBANY
  Wisdom and goodness to the vile seem vile;
  Filths savour but themselves. What have you done,
  Tigers not daughters, what have you performed?
  A father, and a gracious agèd man,
  Whose reverence even the head-lugged bear would lick,
  Most barbarous, most degenerate, have you madded.
  Could my good brother suffer you to do it?
  A man, a prince, by him so benefited.
  If the heavens do not their visible spirits
  Send quickly down to tame these vile offences,
  It will come—
  Humanity must perforce prey on itself
  Like monsters of the deep.
GONERIL   Milk-livered man!
  That bear a cheek for blows, a head for wrongs!
  Who have not in your brows an eye discerning
  Your honour from your suffering, that not know
  Fools do those villains pity who are punished
  Ere they have done their mischief. Where's your
    drum?
  France spreads his banners in our noiseless land,

With plumèd helm. Your state begins to threaten,
While you, a moral fool, sit still and cry
'Alas, why does he so?'
ALBANY   See yourself, devil!
Proper deformity shows not in the fiend
So horrid as in woman.
GONERIL   O vain fool!
ALBANY
You changèd and self-covered thing, for shame,
Be-monster not your feature. Were it my fitness
To let these hands obey my blood,
They are apt enough to dislocate and tear
Your flesh and bones. However you are a fiend,
A woman's shape does shield you.
GONERIL   For sure, your manhood! Mew!

Enter a MESSENGER

ALBANY   What news?
MESSENGER
O, my good lord, the Duke of Cornwall's dead,
Slain by his servant, going to put out
The other eye of Gloucester.
ALBANY   Gloucester's eyes?
MESSENGER
A servant that he bred, thrilled with remorse,
Opposed against the act, bending his sword
To his great master; who, thereat enraged,
Flew on him and among them felled him dead,
But not without that harmful stroke which since
Has plucked him after.
ALBANY   This shows you are above,
You justicers, that these our nether crimes
So speedily can venge! But, O, poor Gloucester!
Lost he his other eye?

MESSENGER   Both, both, my lord.
  This letter, madam, craves a speedy answer.
  'Tis from your sister.
GONERIL *(aside)*   One way I like this well.
  But being widow, and my Gloucester with her,
  May all the building in my fancy pluck
  Upon my hateful life. Another way
  The news is not so tart.—*(Aloud)* I'll read and
    answer.   *Exit*
ALBANY
  Where was his son when they did take his eyes?
MESSENGER
  Come with my lady hither.
ALBANY   He is not here.
MESSENGER
  No, my good lord; I met him back again.
ALBANY   Knows he the wickedness?
MESSENGER
  Ay, my good lord. 'Twas he informed against him,
  And quit the house on purpose that their punishment
  Might have the freer course.
ALBANY   Gloucester, I live
  To thank you for the love you showed the King
  And to revenge your eyes. Come hither, friend;
  Tell me what more you know.   *Exeunt*

SCENE III
The French camp, near Dover.

Enter KENT *and a* GENTLEMAN

KENT   Why the King of France has so suddenly gone
  back, know you no reason?

GENTLEMAN   Something he left imperfect in the state,
   which since his coming forth is thought of: which
   imports to the kingdom so much fear and danger
   that his personal return was most required and
   necessary.

KENT   Whom has he left behind him general?

GENTLEMAN   The Marshal of France, Monsieur La Far.

KENT   Did your letters pierce the Queen to any
   demonstration of grief?

GENTLEMAN

   Ay, sir; she took them, read them in my presence,
   And now and then an ample tear trilled down
   Her delicate cheek. It seemed she was a queen
   Over her passion which, most rebel-like,
   Sought to be king over her.

KENT   O, then it moved her?

GENTLEMAN

   Not to a rage; patience and sorrow strove
   Which should express her goodliest. You have seen
   Sunshine and rain at once; her smiles and tears
   Were like a better way. Those happy smilets
   That played on her ripe lip seem not to know
   What guests were in her eyes, which parted thence
   As pearls from diamonds dropped. In brief,
   Sorrow would be a rarity most beloved
   If all could so become it.

KENT   Made she no verbal question?

GENTLEMAN

   Faith, once or twice she heaved the name of father
   Pantingly forth, as if it pressed her heart,
   Cried 'Sisters! Sisters! Shame of ladies! Sisters!
   Kent! Father! Sisters!—What, in storm? at night?
   Let pity not be believed!' There she shook
   The holy water from her heavenly eyes,

And clamour-moistened; then away she started
To deal with grief alone.

KENT   It is the stars,
The stars above us govern our conditions.
Else one self mate and make could not beget
Such different issues. You spoke not with her since?

GENTLEMAN   No.

KENT
Was this before the King returned?

GENTLEMAN   No, since.

KENT
Well, sir, the poor distressèd Lear's in the town,
Who sometimes in his better tune remembers
What we are come about, and by no means
Will yield to see his daughter.

GENTLEMAN   Why, good sir?

KENT
A sovereign shame so elbows him: his own
    unkindness
That stripped her from his benediction, turned her
To foreign casualties, gave her dear rights
To his dog-hearted daughters. These things sting
His mind so venomously that burning shame
Detains him from Cordelia.

GENTLEMAN   Alas, poor gentleman!

KENT
Of Albany's and Cornwall's armies you heard not?

GENTLEMAN   'Tis so. They are afoot.

KENT
Well, sir, I'll bring you to our master Lear
And leave you to attend him. Some dear cause
Will in concealment wrap me up awhile.
When I am known aright you shall not grieve
Lending me this acquaintance. I pray you
Go along with me.   *Exeunt*

SCENE IV
The same.

Enter, with drum and colours, CORDELIA, DOCTOR, *and soldiers*

CORDELIA

Alas, 'tis he! Why, he was met even now
As mad as the vexed sea, singing aloud,
Crowned with fumitory and furrow-weeds,
With burdocks, hemlock, nettles, cuckoo-flowers,
Darnel, and all the idle weeds that grow
In our sustaining corn. *(To soldiers)* A century send
  forth;
Search every acre in the high-grown field
And bring him to our eye.   *Exeunt soldiers*
(To Doctor)   What can man's wisdom
In the restoring his bereavèd sense?
He that helps him, take all my outward worth.

DOCTOR

There is means, madam.
Our foster-nurse of nature is repose,
Which he lacks; and that to provoke in him
Are many simples operative, whose power
Will close the eye of anguish.

CORDELIA   All blest secrets,
All you unpublished virtues of the earth,
Spring with my tears! Be aidant and remediate
In the good man's distress. Seek, seek for him,
Lest his ungoverned rage dissolves the life
That wants the means to lead it.

Enter a MESSENGER

MESSENGER   News, madam:
The British forces are marching hitherward.

CORDELIA

  'Tis known before. Our preparation stands
  In expectation of them. O dear father,
  It is your business that I go about.
  Therefore great France
  My mourning and importuned tears has pitied.
  No blown ambition does our arms incite
  But love, dear love, and our aged father's right.
  Soon may I hear and see him!   *Exeunt*

SCENE V
Gloucester's castle.

Enter REGAN *and* OSWALD

REGAN

  But are my brother's forces set forth?

OSWALD   Ay, madam.

REGAN

  Himself in person there?

OSWALD   Madam, with much ado.

  Your sister is the better soldier.

REGAN

  Lord Edmund spoke not with your lord at home?

OSWALD No, madam.

REGAN

  What might import my sister's letter to him?

OSWALD I know not, lady.

REGAN

  Faith, he is posted hence on serious matter.
  It was great ignorance, Gloucester's eyes being out,
  To let him live. Where he arrives he moves
  All hearts against us. Edmund, I think, is gone,
  In pity of his misery, to dispatch
  His nighted life—moreover to descry
  The strength of the enemy.

OSWALD

   I must needs after him, madam, with my letter.

REGAN

   Our troops set forth tomorrow; stay with us.

   The ways are dangerous.

OSWALD   I may not, madam.

   My lady charged my duty in this business.

REGAN

   Why should she write to Edmund? Might not you

   Transport her purposes by word? Perhaps—

   Some things—I know not what—I'll love you much—

   Let me unseal the letter.

OSWALD   Madam, I had rather—

REGAN

   I know your lady does not love her husband—

   I am sure of that—and at her late being here

   She gave strange glances and most speaking looks

   To noble Edmund. I know you are of her bosom.

OSWALD   I, madam?

REGAN

   I speak in understanding. You are; I know it.

   Therefore I do advise you take this note:

   My lord is dead; Edmund and I have talked,

   And more convenient is he for my hand

   Than for your lady's. You may gather more.

   If you do find him, pray you give him this;

   And when your mistress hears thus much from you,

   I pray desire her call her wisdom to her.

   So fare you well.

   If you do chance to hear of that blind traitor,

   Preferment falls on him that cuts him off.

OSWALD

   Would I could meet him, madam! I should show

   What party I do follow.

REGAN   Fare you well.   *Exeunt*

SCENE VI
The country near Dover.

Enter GLOUCESTER *and* EDGAR *in peasant's clothes*

GLOUCESTER
  When shall I come to the top of that same hill?
EDGAR
  You do climb up it now. Look how we labour.
GLOUCESTER
  I think the ground is even.
EDGAR   Horrible steep.
  Hark, do you hear the sea?
GLOUCESTER   No, truly.
EDGAR
  Why then your other senses grow imperfect
  By your eyes' anguish.
GLOUCESTER   So may it be indeed.
  I think your voice is altered, and you speak
  In better phrase and matter than you did.
EDGAR
  You are deceived. In nothing am I changed
  But in my garments.
GLOUCESTER   I think you are better spoken.
EDGAR
  Come on, sir; here's the place. Stand still! How
      fearful
  And dizzy 'tis to cast one's eyes so low!
  The crows and choughs that wing the midway air
  Show scarce so gross as beetles. Halfway down
  Hangs one that gathers samphire—dreadful trade!
  I think he seems no bigger than his head.
  The fishermen that walk upon the beach
  Appear like mice, and yon tall anchoring bark
  Diminished to her cock; her cock, a buoy

Almost too small for sight. The murmuring surge
That on the unnumbered idle pebble chafes
Cannot be heard so high. I'll look no more,
Lest my brain turns, and the deficient sight
Topples down headlong.

GLOUCESTER   Set me where you stand.

EDGAR

Give me your hand. You are now within a foot
Of the extreme verge. For all beneath the moon
Would I not leap upright.

GLOUCESTER   Let go my hand.

Here, friend, is another purse; in it a jewel
Well worth a poor man's taking. Fairies and gods
Prosper it with you! Go you further off.
Bid me farewell; and let me hear you going.

EDGAR

Now fare you well, good sir.

GLOUCESTER   With all my heart.

EDGAR   *(aside)*

Why I do trifle thus with his despair
Is done to cure it.

GLOUCESTER   *(kneeling)* O you mighty gods!
This world I do renounce, and in your sights
Shake patiently my great affliction off.
If I could bear it longer and not fall
To quarrel with your irresistible wills,
My wick and loathèd part of nature should
Burn itself out. If Edgar lives, O bless him!
Now, fellow, fare you well.

EDGAR   Gone, sir. Farewell.

GLOUCESTER *falls forward*

And yet I know not how fancy may rob
The treasury of life, when life itself

Yields to the theft. Had he been where he thought,
By this had thought been past.—Alive or dead?
Ho, you, sir! Friend! Hear you, sir? Speak!—
Thus might he pass indeed. Yet he revives—
What are you, sir?

GLOUCESTER   Away, and let me die.

EDGAR

Had you been aught but gossamer, feathers, air,
So many fathom down precipitating,
You'd shivered like an egg; but you do breathe,
Have heavy substance, bleed not, speak, are sound.
Ten masts at each make not the altitude
Which you have perpendicularly fallen.
Your life's a miracle. Speak yet again.

GLOUCESTER   But have I fallen or no?

EDGAR

From the dread summit of this chalky bourn.
Look up a-height. The shrill-gorged lark so far
Cannot be seen or heard. Do but look up.

GLOUCESTER   Alas, I have no eyes.

Is wretchedness deprived that benefit
To end itself by death? 'Twas yet some comfort
When misery could beguile the tyrant's rage
And frustrate his proud will.

EDGAR   Give me your arm.

Up—so. How is it? Feel you your legs? You stand.

GLOUCESTER

Too well, too well.

EDGAR   This is above all strangeness.

Upon the crown of the cliff what thing was that
Which parted from you?

GLOUCESTER   A poor unfortunate beggar.

EDGAR

As I stood here below I thought his eyes
Were two full moons; he had a thousand noses,

Horns welked and waved like the enridgèd sea.
It was some fiend. Therefore, you happy father,
Think that the clearest gods, who make them honours
Of men's impossibilities, have preserved you.

GLOUCESTER

I do remember now. Henceforth I'll bear
Affliction till it does cry out itself
'Enough, enough', and dies. That thing you speak of,
I took it for a man; often it would say
'The fiend, the fiend'; he led me to that place.

EDGAR

Bear free and patient thoughts.

Enter LEAR *bedecked with wild flowers*

                                    But who comes here?
The safer sense will never accommodate
His master thus.

LEAR   No, they cannot touch me for coining. I am the
King himself.

EDGAR   O you side-piercing sight!

LEAR   Nature is above art in that respect. There's your
press-money.—That fellow handles his bow like a
crow-keeper.—Draw me a clothier's yard.—Look,
look, a mouse!—Peace, peace! this piece of toasted
cheese will do it.—There's my gauntlet; I'll prove
it on a giant.—Bring up the brown bills.—O, well
flown, bird! In the bull's-eye, in the bull's eye!
Hewgh!—Give the word.

EDGAR   Sweet marjoram.

LEAR   Pass.

GLOUCESTER   I know that voice.

He falls to his knees

LEAR   Ha! Goneril with a white beard! They flattered
   me like a dog and told me I had the white hairs in
   my beard ere the black ones were there. To say 'ay'
   and 'no' to everything that I said, 'ay' and 'no' too
   was no good divinity. When the rain came to wet
   me once and the wind to make me chatter; when
   the thunder would not peace at my bidding; there I
   found them, there I smelt them out. Go to, they
   are not men of their words. They told me I was
   everything. 'Tis a lie: I am not ague-proof.

GLOUCESTER
   The trick of that voice I do well remember.
   Is it not the King?

LEAR   Ay, every inch a king.
   When I do stare see how the subject quakes.
   I pardon that man's life. What was your cause?
   Adultery?
   You shall not die. Die for adultery? No.
   The wren goes to it, and the small gilded fly
   Does lecher in my sight.
   Let copulation thrive; for Gloucester's bastard son
   Was kinder to his father than my daughters
   Got between the lawful sheets.
   To it, lust, pell-mell, for I lack soldiers.
   Behold yon simpering dame
   Whose face between her forks presages snow,
   That minces virtue and does shake the head
   To hear of pleasure's name—
   The weasel nor the fresh-fed horse goes to it
   With a more riotous appetite.
   Down from the waist they are centaurs,
   Though women all above;
   But to the girdle do the gods inherit,
   Beneath is all the fiends'—

There's hell, there's darkness, there is the
sulphurous pit—burning, scalding, stench,
consumption! Fie, fie, fie! Pah, pah! Give me an
ounce of scent; good apothecary, sweeten my
imagination. There's money for you.

GLOUCESTER   O, let me kiss that hand!

LEAR   Let me wipe it first; it smells of mortality.

GLOUCESTER

O ruined piece of nature! This great world
Shall so wear out to naught. Do you know me?

LEAR   I remember your eyes well enough. Do you
squint at me? No, do your worst, blind Cupid; I'll
not love. Read you this challenge; mark but the
penning of it.

GLOUCESTER

Were all your letters suns, I could not see.

EDGAR   *(aside)*

I would not take this from report. It is;
And my heart breaks at it.

LEAR   Read.

GLOUCESTER   What, with the case of eyes?

LEAR   O, ho, are you there with me? No eyes in your
head, and no money in your purse? Your eyes are in
a heavy case, your purse in a light; yet you see how
this world goes.

GLOUCESTER   I see it feelingly.

LEAR   What, are you mad? A man may see how this
world goes with no eyes. Look with your ears. See
how yon justice rails upon yon simple thief. Hark
in your ear—change places and, handy-dandy,
which is the justice, which is the thief? You have
seen a farmer's dog bark at a beggar?

GLOUCESTER   Ay, sir.

LEAR   If the creature runs from the cur, there you
might behold the great image of authority: a dog is
obeyed in office.

You rascal beadle, hold your bloody hand.
Why do you lash that whore? Strip your own back.
You hotly lust to use her in that kind
For which you whip her. The usurer hangs the
    cozener.
Through tattered clothes great vices do appear;
Robes and furred gowns hide all. Plate [mail] sins with
    gold,
And the strong lance of justice hurtless breaks;
Arm it in rags, a pygmy's straw does pierce it.
None does offend, none, I say none; I'll able them.
Take that of me, my friend, who have the power
To seal the accusers' lips. Get you glass eyes,
And like a scurvy politician seem
To see the things you do not. Now, now, now,
    now!
Pull off my boots. Harder, harder—so.

EDGAR

O matter and impertinency mixed,
Reason in madness!

LEAR

If you will weep my fortunes, take my eyes.
I know you well enough; your name is Gloucester.
You must be patient; we came crying hither.
You know the first time that we smell the air
We wail and cry. I will preach to you—Mark!

He takes off his coronet of flowers

GLOUCESTER   Alas, alas the day!

LEAR

When we are born we cry that we are come
To this great stage of fools.—This is a good block.
It were a delicate stratagem to shoe
A troop of horse with felt. I'll put it in proof;

And when I have stolen upon these son-in-laws,
Then kill, kill, kill, kill, kill, kill!

Enter a GENTLEMAN *and two attendants.*
GLOUCESTER *and* EDGAR *draw back*

GENTLEMAN

O, here he is. Lay hand upon him.—Sir,
Your most dear daughter—

LEAR

No rescue? What, a prisoner? I am even
The natural fool of fortune. Use me well;
You shall have ransom. Let me have surgeons;
I am cut to the brains.

GENTLEMAN   You shall have anything.

LEAR

No seconds? All myself?
Why, this would make a man a man of salt,
To use his eyes for garden water-pots,
Ay, and laying autumn's dust. I will die bravely,
Like a smug bridegroom. What! I will be jovial.
Come, come, I am a king; masters, know you that?

GENTLEMAN

You are a royal one, and we obey you.

LEAR   Then there's life in it. Come, if you get it,
you shall get it by running. Sa, sa, sa, sa.

Exit running, followed by attendants

GENTLEMAN

A sight most pitiful in the meanest wretch,
Past speaking of in a king.—You have one
     daughter
Who redeems nature from the general curse
Which twain have brought her to.

EDGAR *(coming forward)*
  Hail, gentle sir.
GENTLEMAN Sir, speed you; what's your will?
EDGAR
  Do you hear aught, sir, of a battle toward?
GENTLEMAN
  Most sure and common. Everyone hears that
  Who can distinguish sound.
EDGAR   But, by your favour,
  How near is the other army?
GENTLEMAN
  Near, and on speedy foot. The main army
  Stands on the hourly thought.
EDGAR   I thank you, sir; that's all.
GENTLEMAN
  Though now the Queen on special cause is here,
  Her army has moved on.
EDGAR   I thank you, sir.
                                Exit Gentleman
GLOUCESTER *(coming forward)*
  You ever-gentle gods, take my breath from me.
  Let not my worse spirit tempt me again
  To die before you please.
EDGAR   Well pray you, father.
GLOUCESTER Now, good sir, what are you?
EDGAR
  A most poor man made tame to fortune's blows,
  Who, by the art of known and feeling sorrows,
  Am pregnant to good pity. Give me your hand,
  I'll lead you to some biding.
GLOUCESTER   Hearty thanks;
  The bounty and the benison of heaven
  Besides, and more!

                    Enter OSWALD

OSWALD   A proclaimed prize! Most happy!
  That eyeless head of yours was first framed flesh
  To raise my fortunes. You old unhappy traitor,
  Briefly yourself remember; the sword is out
  That must destroy you.
GLOUCESTER   Now let your friendly hand
  Put strength enough to it.

                  EDGAR *intervenes*

OSWALD   Wherefore, bold peasant,
  Dare you support a published traitor? Hence,
  Lest the infection of his fortune takes
  Like hold on you. Let go his arm!
EDGAR
  'Chill not let go, zir, without vurther 'casion. [occasion][1]
OSWALD   Let go, slave, or you die!
EDGAR   Good gentleman, go your gate and let poor
  volk pass. And 'choud ha' bin zwaggered out of my
  life, 'twould not ha' bin zo long as 'tis by a
  vortnight. Nay, come not near th'old man; keep
  out, che vor' ye, or I'ce try whether your costard
  [head] or my cudgel be the harder.
  'Chill be plain with you.
OSWALD   Out, dunghill!
EDGAR   'Chill pick your teeth, zir. Come; no matter
  vor your thrusts.

                  They fight

OSWALD
  Slave, you have slain me. Villain, take my purse.
  If ever you will thrive, bury my body

---

[1] Edgar is here talking South Western dialect, which Elizabethans used for rustic speech on the stage.

And give the letters which you find about me
To Edmund, Earl of Gloucester. Seek him out
Upon the English party. O, untimely
Death!—Death—   *He dies*

EDGAR

I know you well: a serviceable villain,
As duteous to the vices of your mistress
As badness would desire.

GLOUCESTER   What, is he dead?

EDGAR

Sit you down, father; rest you.—
Let's see these pockets. The letters that he speaks
    of
May be my friends. He's dead. I am only sorry
He had no other deathsman. Let us see.
Leave, gentle wax; and manners blame us not;
To know our enemies' minds we rip their hearts;
Their papers are more lawful.

(*He reads the letter*)

Let our reciprocal vows be remembered. You have
many opportunities to cut him off; if your will
wants not, time and place will be fruitfully offered.
There is nothing done if he returns the conqueror.
Then am I the prisoner, and his bed my gaol; from
the loathed warmth whereof deliver me and supply
the place for your labour.

Your—wife, so I would say—affectionate servant,

Goneril.

O undistinguished space of woman's will!
A plot upon her virtuous husband's life,
And the exchange, my brother! Here in the sands

You I'll rake up, the post unsanctified
Of murderous lechers; and in the mature time
With this ungracious paper strike the sight
Of the death-practised Duke. For him it is well
That of your death and business I can tell.

GLOUCESTER

The King is mad; how stiff is my vile sense,
That I stand up and have ingenious feeling
Of my huge sorrows! Better I were distract;
So should my thoughts be severed from my griefs,
And woes by wrong imaginations lose
The knowledge of themselves.

Drum afar off

EDGAR   Give me your hand.
Far off I think I hear the beaten drum.
Come, father, I'll bestow you with a friend.   *Exeunt*

SCENE VII
The French camp: before a tent.

Enter CORDELIA, KENT, *and* DOCTOR

CORDELIA

O you good Kent, how shall I live and work
To match your goodness? My life will be too short
And every measure fail me.

KENT

To be acknowledged, madam, is over-paid.
All my reports go with the modest truth,
Nor more, nor clipped, but so.

CORDELIA   Be better suited.
These garments are memories of those worse
     hours.

I pray you put them off.

KENT   Pardon, dear madam,
Yet to be known shortens my made intent.
My boon I make it that you know me not
Till time and I think meet.

CORDELIA
Then be it so, my good lord.
(To Doctor)   How does the King?

DOCTOR   Madam, sleeps still.

CORDELIA
O you kind gods,
Cure this great breach in his abusèd nature!
The untuned and jarring senses O wind up
Of this child-changèd father.

DOCTOR   So please your majesty,
That we may wake the King. He has slept long.

CORDELIA
Be governed by your knowledge and proceed
In the sway of your own will. Is he arrayed?

DOCTOR
Ay, madam; in the heaviness of sleep
We put fresh garments on him.

> *Enter Gentleman and Lear in a chair*
> *carried by servants*

GENTLEMAN
Be by, good madam, when we do awake him;
I doubt not of his temperance.

CORDELIA   Very well.

> *Music sounds off stage*

DOCTOR
Please you draw near.—Louder the music there!

CORDELIA

  O my dear father! Restoration hang

  Your medicine on my lips; and let this kiss

  Repair those violent harms that my two sisters

  Have in your reverence made.

KENT   Kind and dear princess!

CORDELIA

  Had you not been their father, these white flakes

  Did challenge pity of them. Was this a face

  To be opposed against the jarring winds?

  To stand against the deep dread-bolted thunder,

  In the most terrible and nimble stroke

  Of quick cross lightning? To watch, poor sentinel,

  With this thin helm? My enemy's dog,

  Though he had bitten me, should have stood that

    night

  Against my fire; and were you fain, poor father,

  To hovel you with swine and rogues forlorn

  In short and musty straw? Alas, alas!

  'Tis wonder that your life and wits at once

  Had not concluded all.—He wakes! Speak to him.

DOCTOR   Madam, do you; it is fittest.

CORDELIA

  How does my royal lord? How fares your majesty?

LEAR

  You do me wrong to take me out of the grave.

  You are a soul in bliss; but I am bound

  Upon a wheel of fire, that my own tears

  Do scald like molten lead.

CORDELIA   Sir, do you know me?

LEAR

  You are a spirit, I know. Where did you die?

CORDELIA   Still, still far wide!

DOCTOR

  He's scarce awake. Let him alone awhile.

LEAR

  Where have I been? Where am I? Fair daylight?
  I am mightily abused. I should even die with pity
  To see another thus. I know not what to say.
  I will not swear these are my hands. Let's see.
  I feel this pin-prick. Would I were assured
  Of my condition

CORDELIA   O look upon me, sir,
  And hold your hand in benediction over me.
  No, sir, you must not kneel.

LEAR   Pray do not mock me.
  I am a very foolish fond old man,
  Four score and upward, not an hour more nor less,
  And, to deal plainly,
  I fear I am not in my perfect mind.
  I think I should know you, and know this man;
  Yet I am doubtful; for I am mainly ignorant
  What place this is; and all the skill I have
  Remembers not these garments; and I know not
  Where I did lodge last night. Do not laugh at me,
  For, as I am a man, I think this lady
  To be my child Cordelia.

CORDELIA   And so I am, I am.

LEAR

  Are your tears wet? Yes, faith! I pray, weep not.
  If you have poison for me I will drink it.
  I know you do not love me, for your sisters
  Have, as I do remember, done me wrong.
  You have some cause; they have not.

CORDELIA   No cause, no cause.

LEAR

  Am I in France?

KENT   In your own kingdom, sir.

LEAR   Do not abuse me.

DOCTOR
    Be comforted, good madam. The great rage,
    You see, is killed in him; and yet it is danger
    To make him even o'er the time he has lost.
    Desire him to go in; trouble him no more
    Till further settling.

CORDELIA   Will it please your highness walk?

LEAR   You must bear with me. Pray you now, forget
    and forgive. I am old and foolish.

                 Exeunt all but Kent and Gentleman

GENTLEMAN   Holds it true, sir, that the Duke of
    Cornwall was so slain?

KENT   Most certain, sir.

GENTLEMAN   Who is conductor of his people?

KENT   It is said, the bastard son of Gloucester.

GENTLEMAN   They say Edgar, his banished son, is
    with the Earl of Kent in Germany.

KENT   Report is changeable. It is time to look about.
    The forces of the kingdom approach apace.

GENTLEMAN   The arbitrament is likely to be bloody.
    Fare you well, sir.   *Exit*

KENT
    My point and period will be thoroughly wrought,
    Or well or ill, as this day's battle's fought.   *Exit*

Act V

SCENE I
The British camp, near Dover.

Enter, with drum and colours, EDMUND, REGAN,
gentlemen, and soldiers

EDMUND   *(to a gentleman)*
  Know of the Duke if his last purpose holds
  Or whether since he is advised by aught
  To change the course. *(To Regan)* He's full of
    alteration
  And self-reproving. *(To gentleman)* Bring his
    constant pleasure   *Exit gentleman*

REGAN
  Our sister's man has certainly miscarried.

EDMUND
  It is to be feared, madam.

REGAN   Now, sweet lord,
  You know the goodness I intend upon you.
  Tell me but truly—but then speak the truth—
  Do you not love my sister?

EDMUND   In honoured love.

REGAN
  But have you never found my brother's way
  To the forbidden place?

EDMUND   That thought abuses you.

REGAN
  I am doubtful that you have been conjunct
  And bosomed with her, as far as we call hers.

EDMUND   No, by my honour, madam.

REGAN

   I never shall endure her; dear my lord,

   Be not familiar with her.

EDMUND   Fear not.

   She and the Duke her husband!

Enter, with drum and colours, ALBANY,
Goneril, and soldiers

GONERIL   *(aside)*

   I had rather lose the battle than that sister

   Should loosen him and me.

ALBANY

   Our very loving sister, well be-met.

   Sir, this I heard; the King has come to his daughter,

   With others whom the rigour of our state

   Forced to cry out. Where I could not be honest,

   I never yet was valiant. For this business,

   It touches us as France invades our land,

   Not bolds the King, with others—whom, I fear,

   Most just and heavy causes make oppose.

EDMUND

   Sir, you speak nobly.

REGAN   Why is this reasoned?

GONERIL

   Combine together against the enemy.

   For these domestic and particular broils

   Are not the question here.

ALBANY   Let's then determine

   With the ensign in charge on our proceeding.

EDMUND

   I shall attend you instantly at your tent.

REGAN   Sister, you'll go with us?

GONERIL   No.

REGAN

   It is most convenient. Pray go with us.

GONERIL   *(aside)*
   O, ho, I know the riddle. *(Aloud)* I will go.

Exeunt

As ALBANY *is going out, enter* EDGAR

EDGAR
   If ever your grace had speech with man so poor,
   Hear me one word.
ALBANY   *(To his captains)* I'll overtake you.

(To Edgar) Speak.

EDGAR
   Before you fight the battle, open this letter.
   If you have victory, let the trumpet sound
   For him that brought it. Wretched though I seem,
   I can produce a champion that will prove
   What is affirmed there. If you miscarry,
   Your business of the world has so an end,
   And machination ceases. Fortune love you.
ALBANY
   Stay till I have read the letter.
EDGAR   I was forbidden it.
   When time shall serve, let but the herald cry
   And I'll appear again.   *Exit*
ALBANY
   Why, fare you well. I will overlook your paper.

Enter EDMUND

EDMUND
   The enemy is in view; draw up your troops.
   Here is the guess of their true strength and forces
   By diligent discovery; but your haste
   Is now urged on you.
ALBANY   We will greet the time.   *Exit*

EDMUND

  To both these sisters have I sworn my love;
  Each jealous of the others as the stung
  Are of the adder. Which of them shall I take?
  Both? One? Or neither? Neither can be enjoyed
  If both remain alive. To take the widow
  Exasperates, makes mad, her sister Goneril,
  And hardly shall I carry out my side,
  Her husband being alive. Now then, we'll use
  His countenance for the battle, which being done,
  Let her who would be rid of him devise
  His speedy taking off. As for the mercy
  Which he intends to Lear and to Cordelia,
  The battle done and they within our power,
  Shall never see his pardon; for my state
  Stands on me to defend, not to debate.   *Exit*

SCENE II
A field between the two camps.

Alarum within. Enter, with drum and colours, LEAR,
CORDELIA *holding his hand, and soldiers, over the
stage, and exeunt*
Enter EDGAR *and* GLOUCESTER

EDGAR

  Here, father, take the shadow of this tree
  For your good host. Pray that the right may thrive.
  If ever I return to you again
  I'll bring you comfort.
GLOUCESTER   Grace go with you sir!
                             Exit Edgar

Alarum and retreat within. Enter EDGAR

EDGAR

　Away, old man! Give me your hand; away!
　King Lear has lost; he and his daughter taken.
　Give me your hand; come on.

GLOUCESTER

　No further, sir; a man may rot even here.

EDGAR

　What, in ill thoughts again? Men must endure
　Their going hence even as their coming hither;
　Ripeness is all. Come on.

GLOUCESTER　　　　　　And that's true too.　　　*Exeunt*

SCENE III

The British camp, near Dover.

Enter in conquest with drum and colours
EDMUND; LEAR *and* CORDELIA *as prisoners;*
soldiers, CAPTAIN

EDMUND

　Some officers take them away. Good guard,
　Until their greater pleasures first are known
　That are to censure them

CORDELIA　　　　　　　　We are not the first
　Who with best meaning have incurred the worst.
　For you, oppressèd King, I am cast down;
　Myself could else out-frown false Fortune's frown.
　(To Edmund)
　Shall we not see these daughters and these sisters?

LEAR

　No, no, no, no! Come, let's away to prison.
　We two alone will sing like birds in the cage;
　When you do ask me blessing I'll kneel down
　And ask of you forgiveness; So we'll live,

And pray, and sing, and tell old tales, and laugh
At gilded butterflies, and hear poor rogues
Talk of Court news. And we'll talk with them too—
Who loses and who wins, who's in, who's out—
And take upon us the mystery of things
As if we were God's spies. And we'll wear out,
In a walled prison, packs and sects of great ones
That ebb and flow by the moon.

EDMUND   Take them away.

LEAR

Upon such sacrifices, my Cordelia,
The gods themselves throw incense. Have I caught
    you?
He that parts us shall bring a brand from heaven
And fire us hence like foxes. Wipe your eyes;
The good-years shall devour them, flesh and skin,
Ere they shall make us weep. We'll see them
    starved first.
Come.   *Exeunt Lear and Cordelia, guarded*

EDMUND

Come hither, captain Hark.
Take you this note; go follow them to prison.
One step I have advanced you; if you do
As this instructs you, you do make your way
To noble fortunes. Know you this, that men
Are as the time is; to be tender-minded
Does not become a sword. Your great employment
Will not bear question; either say you'll do it
Or thrive by other means

CAPTAIN   I'll do it, my lord.

EDMUND

About it; and write happy when you have done.
Mark, I say 'instantly'; and carry it so
As I have set it down.

CAPTAIN

    I cannot draw a cart nor eat dried oats;
    If it is man's work, I'll do it.   *Exit*

Flourish. Enter ALBANY, GONERIL, REGAN, *and officers*

ALBANY

    Sir, you have shown today your valiant strain,
    And Fortune led you well. You have the captives
    Who were the opposites of this day's strife.
    I do require them of you, so to use them
    As we shall find their merits and our safety
    May equally determine.

EDMUND   Sir, I thought it fit

    To send the old and miserable King
    To some retention and appointed guard:
    Whose age had charms in it, whose title more,
    To pluck the common bosom on his side
    And turn our impressed lances in our eyes
    Which do command them. With him I sent the
      Queen,
    My reason all the same; and they are ready
    Tomorrow or at further space to appear
    Where you shall hold your session. At this time
    We sweat and bleed; the friend has lost his friend,
    And the best quarrels in the heat are cursed
    By those that feel their sharpness.
    The question of Cordelia and her father
    Requires a fitter place.

ALBANY   Sir, by your patience,

    I hold you but a subject of this war,
    Not as a brother.

REGAN   That's as we list to grace him.

    I think our pleasure might have been demanded

Ere you had spoken so far. He led our forces,
Bore the commission of my place and person,
Which immediacy may well stand up
And call itself your brother.

GONERIL   Not so hot!
In his own grace he does exalt himself
More than in your addition.

REGAN   In my rights,
By me invested, he does equal the best.

ALBANY
That were the most if he should husband you.

REGAN
Jesters do oft prove prophets.

GONERIL   Holla, Holla!
That eye that told you so looked but asquint.

REGAN
Lady, I am not well; else I should answer
From a full-flowing stomach. (*To Edmund*) General,
Take you my soldiers, prisoners, patrimony,
Dispose of them, of me; the walls are yours.
Witness the world that I create you here
My lord and master.

GONERIL   Mean you to enjoy him?

ALBANY
The let-alone lies not in your good will.

EDMUND
Nor in yours, lord.

ALBANY   Half-blooded fellow, yes.

REGAN (*to Edmund*)
Let the drum strike and prove my title yours.

ALBANY
Stay yet; hear reason. Edmund, I arrest you
On capital treason, and on your account,
This gilded serpent. For your claim, fair sister,
I bar it in the interest of my wife.

'Tis she is sub-contracted to this lord,
And I her husband contradict your banns.
If you will marry, make your love to me;
My lady is bespoken.

GONERIL   An interlude!

ALBANY
You are armed, Gloucester; let the trumpet sound.
If none appears to prove upon your person
Your heinous, manifest, and many treasons,
There is my pledge.

He throws down his glove

                    I'll make it on your heart,
Ere I taste bread, you are in nothing less
Than I have here proclaimed you.

REGAN   Sick, O sick!

GONERIL *(aside)*
If not, I'll never trust medicine.

EDMUND *(throwing down his glove)*
There's my exchange. What in the world he is
That names me traitor, villain-like he lies.
Call by your trumpet. He that dares approach,
On him, on you—who not?—I will maintain
My truth and honour firmly.

ALBANY   A herald, ho!

Enter a Herald

Trust to your single virtue; for your soldiers,
All levied in my name, have in my name
Taken their discharge.

REGAN   My sickness grows upon me.

ALBANY

    She is not well. Convey her to my tent.

                         Exit Regan, supported

    Come hither, herald; let the trumpet sound,

    And read out this.

A trumpet sounds

HERALD   *(reading) If any man of quality or degree*
within the lists of the army will maintain upon
Edmund, supposed Earl of Gloucester, that he is a
manifold traitor, let him appear by the third sound
of the trumpet. He is bold in his defence.

(First trumpet)

    Again!

(Second trumpet)

    Again!

Third trumpet
Trumpet answers within. Enter EDGAR *armed,*
a trumpet before him

ALBANY

    Ask him his purposes, why he appears

    Upon this call of the trumpet.

HERALD   What are you?

    Your name, your quality, and why you answer

    This present summons?

EDGAR   Know, my name is lost,

    By treason's tooth bare-gnawn and worm-eaten.

    Yet am I noble as the adversary

    I come to match.

ALBANY   **Who is that adversary?**

EDGAR

What's he that speaks for Edmund, Earl of Gloucester?

EDMUND

Himself. What say you to him?

EDGAR   Draw your sword,
That if my speech offends a noble heart
Your arm may do you justice. Here is mine.

He draws his sword

Behold; it is the privilege of my honours,
My oath, and my profession. I protest,
Despite your strength, place, youth, and eminence,
Despite your victor sword and fire-new fortune,
Your valour and your heart, you are a traitor,
False to your gods, your brother, and your father,
Conspirant against this high illustrious prince.
And, from the extremest upward of your head
To the descent and dust below your foot,
A most toad-spotted traitor. Say you 'no',
This sword, this arm, and my best spirits are bent
To prove upon your heart, whereto I speak,
You lie.

EDMUND   In wisdom I should ask your name;
But since your outside looks so fair and warlike
And since your tongue some touch of breeding
    breathes,
What safe and nicely I might well delay
By rule of knighthood, I disdain and spurn.
Back do I toss these treasons to your head,
With the hell-hated lie o'erwhelm your heart,
Which, since they yet glance by and scarcely bruise,
This sword of mine shall give them instant way
Where they shall rest for ever. Trumpets, speak!

Alarums. They fight. EDMUND *falls*

ALBANY
  Save him, save him!
GONERIL   This is trickery, Gloucester.
  By the law of war you were not bound to answer
  An unknown opposite. You are not vanquished,
  But cozened and beguiled.
ALBANY   Shut your mouth, dame,
  Or with this paper shall I stop it.—Hold, sir!
  (To Goneril)
  You worse than any name, read your own evil.
  No tearing, lady! I perceive you know it.
GONERIL
  Say if I do; the laws are mine, not yours.
  Who can arraign me for it?
ALBANY   Most monstrous! O!
  (To Edmund)
  Know you this paper?
EDMUND   Ask me not what I know.
                                            Exit Goneril

ALBANY
  Go after her. She's desperate. Govern her.
                                        Exit First Officer
EDMUND
  What you have charged me with, that have I done,
  And more, much more; the time will bring it out.
  'Tis past; and so am I. But what are you
  That have this fortune on me? If you are noble,
  I do forgive you.
EDGAR   Let's exchange charity.
  I am no less in blood than you are, Edmund;
  If more, the more you've wronged me.

My name is Edgar, and your father's son.
The gods are just, and of our pleasant vices
Make instruments to plague us:
The dark and vicious place where you he got
Cost him his eyes.
EDMUND   You have spoken right. 'Tis true.
The wheel is come full circle; I am here.
ALBANY
I thought your very gait did prophesy
A royal nobleness. I must embrace you.
Let sorrow split my heart if ever I
Did hate you or your father.
EDGAR   Worthy prince,
I know it.
ALBANY   Where have you hidden yourself?
How have you known the miseries of your father?
EDGAR
By nursing them, my lord. List a brief tale;
And when 'tis told, O that my heart would burst!
The bloody proclamation to escape
That followed me so near—O, our life's sweetness,
That we the pain of death would hourly die
Rather than die at once—taught me to shift
Into a madman's rags, to assume a semblance
That very dogs disdained. And in this habit
Met I my father with his bleeding rings,
Their precious stones new lost; became his guide,
Led him, begged for him, saved him from despair,
Never—O fault!—revealed myself unto him
Until some half hour past. When I was armed,
Not sure, though hoping, of this good success
I asked his blessing, and from first to last
Told him my pilgrimage. But his flawed heart—

Alas, too weak the conflict to support—
Between two extremes of passion, joy and grief,
Burst smilingly.
EDMUND   This speech of yours has moved me,
And shall perchance do good. But speak you on;
You look as you had something more to say.
ALBANY
If there is more, more woeful, hold it in;
For I am almost ready to dissolve,
Hearing of this.
EDGAR   This would have seemed a period
To such as love not sorrow; but another
To amplify too much would make much more
And top extremity.
While I was big in clamour, came there in a man,
Who, having seen me in my worst estate,
Shunned my abhorred society. But then finding
Who 'twas that so endured, with his strong arms
He fastened on my neck and bellowed out
As he'd burst heaven, threw him on my father,
Told the most piteous tale of Lear and him
That ever ear received. Which in recounting
His grief grew overpowering, the strings of life
Began to crack. Twice then the trumpets sounded,
And there I left him tranced.
ALBANY   But who was this?
EDGAR
Kent, sir, the banished Kent, who, in disguise,
Followed his enemy King and did him service
Improper for a slave.

Enter a GENTLEMAN *with a bloody knife*

GENTLEMAN
Help, help! O, help!

EDGAR   What kind of help?
ALBANY   Speak, man.
EDGAR

What means this bloody knife?
GENTLEMAN   'Tis hot; it smokes!

It came even from the heart of—O, she's dead!
ALBANY   Who dead? Speak, man.
GENTLEMAN

Your lady, sir; your lady! And her sister
By her is poisoned; she confesses it.
EDMUND

I was contracted to them both. All three
Now marry in an instant.
EDGAR   Here comes Kent.

Enter KENT

ALBANY

Produce the bodies, whether alive or dead.
                                   Exit Gentleman
This judgement of the heavens that makes us tremble
Touches us not with pity. (*To Kent*) O, is this he?
The time will not allow the compliment
Which very manners urge.
KENT   I am come

To bid my King and master aye good night.
Is he not here?
ALBANY   Great thing of us forgotten.

Speak, Edmund, where's the King? and where's
    Cordelia?

GONERIL'S *and* REGAN'S *bodies are brought in*

See you this object, Kent?
KENT

Alas, why thus?

EDMUND   Yet Edmund was beloved.
  The one the other poisoned for my sake
  And after slew herself.
ALBANY   Even so. Cover their faces.
EDMUND
  I pant for life; some good I mean to do
  Despite of my own nature. Quickly send—
  Be brief in it—to the castle, for my writ
  Is on the life of Lear and on Cordelia.
  Nay, send in time!
ALBANY   Run, run, O run!
EDGAR
  To whom, my lord? Who has the office? Send
  Your token of reprieve.
EDMUND
  Well thought of. (*To Second Officer*) Take my sword,
  Give it the captain.
EDGAR   Haste you for your life.
                              Exit Second Officer
EDMUND
  He has commission from your wife and me
  To hang Cordelia in the prison, and
  To lay the blame upon her own despair,
  That she fordid herself.
ALBANY
  The gods defend her. Bear him hence awhile.
                              Edmund is borne off

        Enter LEAR *with* CORDELIA *dead in his arms,*
        followed by Second Officer and others

LEAR
  Howl, howl, howl! O, you are men of stones!
  Had I your tongues and eyes I'd use them so
  That heaven's vault should crack. She's gone for ever.

I know when one is dead and when one lives;
She's dead as earth. Lend me a looking-glass;
If her breath will mist or stain the stone,
Why then she lives.

KENT   Is this the promised end?

EDGAR
  Or image of that horror?

ALBANY   Fall and cease!

LEAR
  This feather stirs—she lives! If it is so,
  It is a chance which does redeem all sorrows
  That ever I have felt.

KENT   O my good master!

LEAR
  Pray you, away.

EDGAR   'Tis noble Kent, your friend.

LEAR
  A plague upon you, murderers, traitors all!
  I might have saved her; now she's gone for ever.
  Cordelia, Cordelia, stay a little. Ha!
  What is it you say? Her voice was ever soft,
  Gentle and low—an excellent thing in woman.
  I killed the slave that was a-hanging you.

SECOND OFFICER
  'Tis true, my lords; he did.

LEAR   Did I not, fellow?
  I have seen the day, with my good biting sword
  I would have made him skip. I am old now
  And these same crosses spoil me.—Who are you?
  My eyes are not of the best, I'll tell you straight.

KENT
  If Fortune brag of two she loved and hated
  One of them we behold.

LEAR
  This is a dull sight. Are you not Kent?

KENT   The same—
  Your servent Kent. Where is your servant Caius?

LEAR
  He's a good fellow, I can tell you that;
  He'll strike, and quickly too. He's dead and rotten.

KENT
  No, my good lord; I am the very man—

LEAR   I'll see that straight.

KENT
  That from your first of difference and decay
  Have followed your sad steps—

LEAR   You are welcome hither.

KENT
  Nor any man else. All's cheerless, dark, and deadly.
  Your eldest daughters have fordone themselves,
  And desperately are dead.

LEAR   Ay, so I think.

ALBANY
  He knows not what he sees, and vain is it
  That we present us to him.

EDGAR   Very fruitless.

Enter a MESSENGER

MESSENGER
  Edmund is dead, my lord.

ALBANY   That's but a trifle here.
  You lords and noble friends, know our intent:
  What comfort to this great decay may come
  Shall be applied. For us, we will resign
  During the life of this old majesty
  To him our absolute power.
  (*To Edgar and Kent*)   You to your rights
  With more, and such addition as your honours
  Have more than merited. All friends shall taste
  The wages of their virtue, and all foes

The cup of their deservings.—O, see, see!
LEAR
  And my poor fool is hanged! No, no, no life!
  Why should a dog, a horse, a rat have life,
  And you no breath at all? You'll come no more;
  Never, never, never, never, never.
  Pray you undo this button. Thank you, sir.
  Do you see this? Look on her! Look, her lips!
  Look there! Look there!   *He dies*
EDGAR   He faints. My lord, my lord!
KENT
  Break, heart; I pray you, break.
EDGAR   Look up, my lord.
KENT
  Vex not his ghost. O, let him pass. He hates him
  That would upon the rack of this tough world
  Stretch him out longer.
EDGAR   He is gone indeed.
KENT
  The wonder is he has endured so long.
  He but usurped his life.
ALBANY
  Bear them from hence. Our present business
  Is general woe.
  (To Kent and Edgar)
            Friends of my soul, you twain,
  Rule in this realm, and the gored state sustain.
KENT
  I have a journey, sir, shortly to go.
  My master calls me, I must not say no.
EDGAR
  The weight of this sad time we must obey;
  Speak what we feel, not what we ought to say.
  The oldest has borne most; we that are young
  Shall never see so much nor live so long.

                   Exeunt with a dead march